MCAT QUICKSHEETS

BEHAVIORAL SCIENCES

BIOLOGY AND BEHA

Organization of the Nervous System

The three types of neurons in the nervous system are motor (efferent), interneurons, and sensory (afferent).

The **parasympathetic** branch of the autonomic system is focused on "rest-and-digest" responses and the **sympathetic** branch is focused on "fight-or-flight" responses.

Parasympathetic System

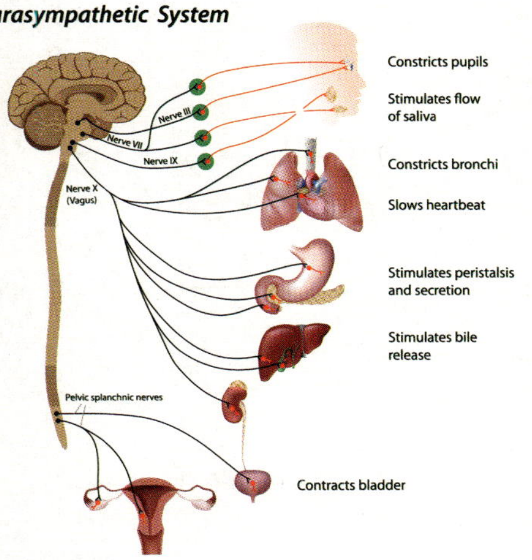

Sympathetic System

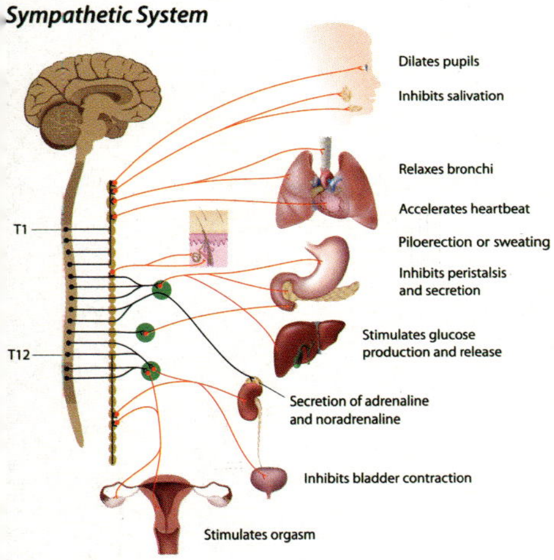

Organization of the Brain

- **Hindbrain:** contains the cerebellum, medulla oblongata, and reticular formation
- **Midbrain:** contains the inferior and superior colliculi
- **Forebrain:** contains the thalamus, hypothalamus, basal ganglia, limbic system, and cerebral cortex

Parts of the Forebrain

- **Thalamus:** relay station for sensory information
- **Hypothalamus:** maintains homeostasis and integrates with the endocrine system through the **hypophyseal portal system** that connects it to the **anterior pituitary**
- **Basal ganglia:** smoothens movements and helps maintain postural stability
- **Limbic system:** controls emotion and memory. Includes **septal nuclei** (pleasure-seeking), **amygdala** (fear and aggression), **hippocampus** (memory), and **fornix** (communication within limbic system).

The **cerebral cortex** is divided into four lobes.

Lobe	Function
Frontal	Executive function, impulse control, long-term planning (prefrontal cortex), motor function (primary motor cortex), speech production (Broca's area)
Parietal	Sensation of touch, pressure, temperature, and pain (somatosensory cortex); spatial processing, orientation, and manipulation
Occipital	Visual processing
Temporal	Sound processing (auditory cortex), speech perception (Wernicke's area), memory, and emotion (limbic system)

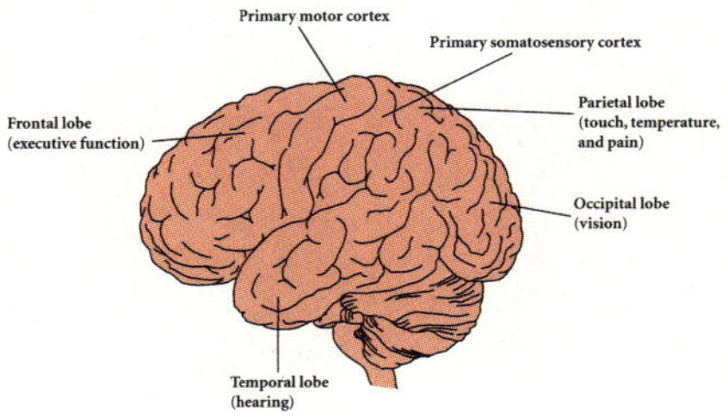

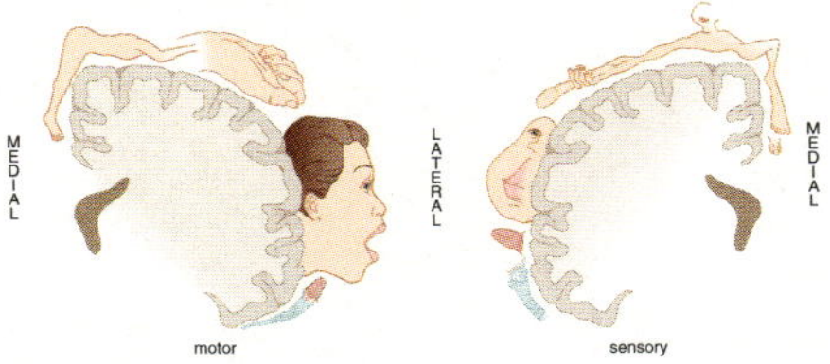

Influences on Behavior

Neurotransmitter	Behavior
Acetylcholine	Voluntary muscle control, parasympathetic nervous system, attention, alertness
Epinephrine and Norepinephrine	Fight-or-flight responses, wakefulness, alertness
Dopamine	Smooth movements, postural stability
Serotonin	Mood, sleep, eating, dreaming
GABA, Glycine	Brain "stabilization"
Glutamate	Brain "excitation"
Endorphins	Natural painkillers

Nature *vs.* nurture is a debate regarding the contributions of genetics (nature) and environment (nurture) to an individual's traits. Family, twin, and adoption studies are used to study nature *vs.* nurture.

SENSATION AND PERCEPTION

Sensation *vs.* Perception

Sensation is the conversion of physical stimuli into neurological signals, while **perception** is the processing of sensory information to make sense of its significance.

- **Sensory receptors** respond to stimuli and trigger electrical signals.
- Sensory neurons transmit information from sensory receptors to the CNS.
- Sensory stimuli are transmitted to **projection areas** in the brain, which further analyze the sensory input.

Threshold: the minimum stimulus that causes a change in signal transduction

Weber's law: states that the just-noticeable difference for a stimulus is proportional to the magnitude of the stimulus, and this proportion is constant over most of the range of possible stimuli

Signal detection theory: studies the effects of nonsensory factors, such as experiences, motives, and expectations, on perception of stimuli

	Subject's Response: "Yes"	Subject's Response: "No"
Signal Present	Hit	Miss
Signal Absent	False alarm	Correct negative

Response bias: examined using signal detection experiments with four possible outcomes: hits, misses, false alarms, and correct negatives

Adaptation: a decrease in response to a stimulus over time

Vision

The eye is an organ specialized to detect light in the form of photons.

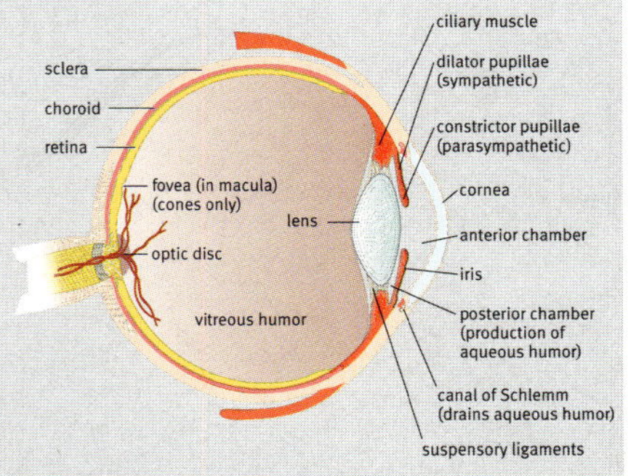

Visual pathway: retina → optic nerve → optic chiasm → optic tracts → lateral geniculate nucleus (LGN) of thalamus → visual radiations → visual cortex

Hearing and Vestibular Sense

The ear transduces sound waves into electrical signals that can be interpreted by the brain.

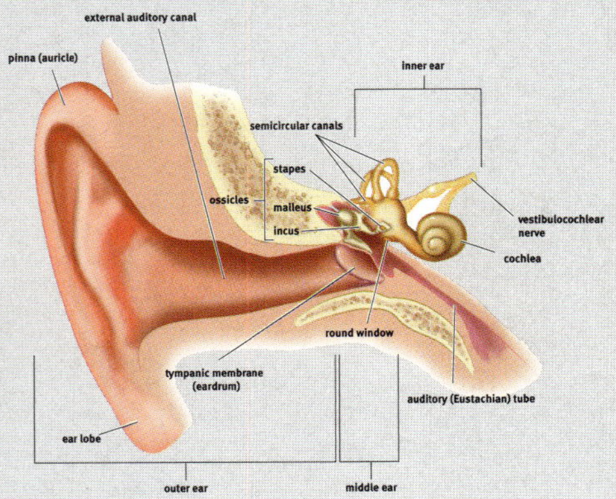

- **Cochlea:** detects sound
- **Utricle** and **saccule:** detect linear acceleration
- **Semicircular canals:** detect rotational acceleration

Auditory pathway: cochlea → vestibulocochlear nerve → medial geniculate nucleus (MGN) of thalamus → auditory cortex

Other Senses

- **Smell:** detection of volatile or aerosolized chemicals by **olfactory chemoreceptors (olfactory nerves)**
- **Taste:** detection of dissolved compounds by **taste buds** in **papillae**
- **Somatosensation:** four touch modalities (pressure, vibration, pain, and temperature)
- **Kinesthetic sense (proprioception):** ability to tell where one's body is in space

Object Recognition

- **Bottom-up (data-driven) processing:** recognition of objects by parallel processing and feature detection. Slower, but less prone to mistakes
- **Top-down (conceptually-driven) processing:** recognition of an object by memories and expectations, with little attention to detail. Faster, but more prone to mistakes
- **Gestalt principles:** ways that the brain can infer missing parts of an image when it is incomplete

LEARNING AND MEMORY

Learning

- **Habituation:** the process of becoming used to a stimulus
- **Dishabituation:** occurs when a second stimulus intervenes, causing a **resensitization** to the original stimulus
- **Observational learning:** the acquisition of behavior by watching others
- **Associative learning:** pairing together stimuli and responses, or behaviors and consequences
- **Classical conditioning:** a form of associative learning in which a neutral stimulus becomes associated with an **unconditioned stimulus** such that the neutral stimulus alone produces the same response as the unconditioned stimulus; the neutral stimulus thus becomes a **conditioned stimulus**

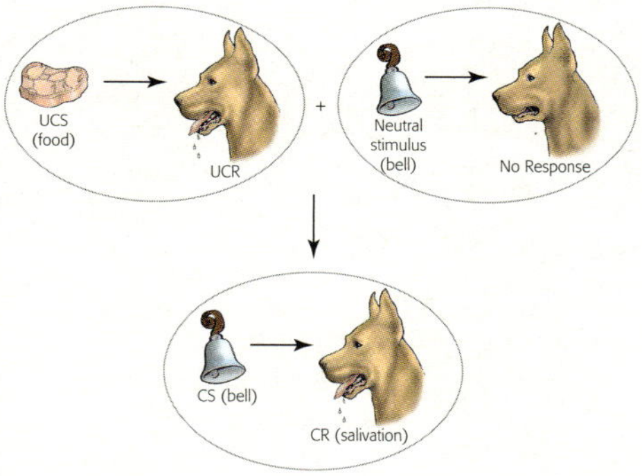

- **Operant conditioning:** a form of associative learning in which the frequency of a behavior is modified using **reinforcement** (increases behavior) or **punishment** (decreases behavior)

		Stimulus	
		Added	Removed
Behavior	Continues	Positive reinforcement	Negative reinforcement
	Stops	Positive punishment	Negative punishment

COGNITION, CONSCIOUSNESS, AND LANGUAGE

Consciousness

Stage	EEG Waves	Features
Awake	Beta and alpha	Able to perceive, process, access, and express information
1	Theta	Light sleep
2	Theta	Sleep spindles and K complexes
3/4	Delta	Slow-wave sleep; dreams; declarative memory consolidation; some sleep disorders
REM	Mostly beta	Appears awake physiologically; dreams; paralyzed; procedural memory consolidation; some sleep disorders

Sleep disorders include **dyssomnias** (amount or timing of sleep), such as insomnia, narcolepsy, sleep apnea, and sleep deprivation; and **parasomnias** (odd behaviors during sleep), such as night terrors and sleepwalking (somnambulism).

Consciousness-Altering Drugs

Drug addiction is mediated by the **mesolimbic pathway**, which includes the **nucleus accumbens, medial forebrain bundle**, and **ventral tegmental area**. Dopamine is the main neurotransmitter.

Drug Group	Function
Depressants (alcohol, barbiturates, benzodiazepines)	Sense of relaxation and reduced anxiety
Stimulants (amphetamines, cocaine, ecstasy)	Increased arousal
Opiates/opioids (heroin, morphine, opium, pain pills)	Decreased reaction to pain; euphoria
Hallucinogens (LSD, peyote, mescaline, ketamine, psilocybin-containing mushrooms)	Distortions of reality and fantasy; introspection

Marijuana has some features of depressants, stimulants, and hallucinogens (in very high doses).

Memory

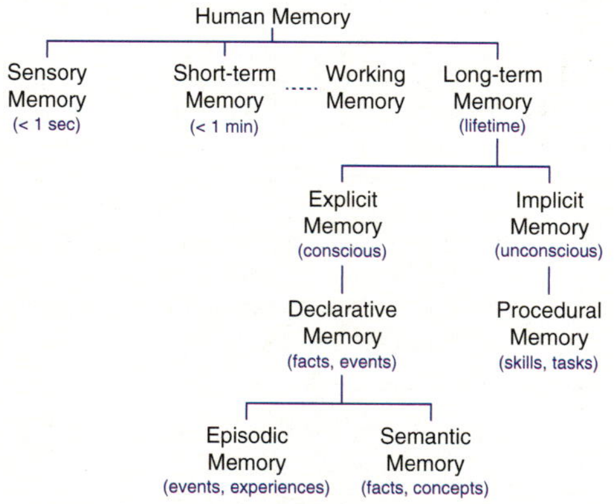

- **Encoding:** the process of putting new information into memory

Facts are stored via **semantic networks. Retrieval** of information is often based on **priming** interconnected nodes of the semantic network.

Recognition of information is stronger than **recall**.

Piaget's Stages of Cognitive Development

- **Sensorimotor stage:** focuses on manipulating the environment to meet physical needs through **circular reactions; object permanence** ends this stage
- **Preoperational stage:** focuses on **symbolic thinking, egocentrism** (inability to imagine what another person thinks or feels), and **centration** (focusing on only one aspect of a phenomenon)
- **Concrete operational stage:** focuses on understanding the feelings of others and manipulating physical (concrete) objects
- **Formal operational stage:** focuses on abstract thought and problem-solving

Problem-Solving and Decision-Making

Problem-solving techniques include **trial-and-error, algorithms, deductive reasoning** (deriving conclusions from general rules) and **inductive reasoning** (deriving generalizations from evidence).

Heuristics (simplified principles used to make decisions, "rules of thumb"), biases, intuition, and emotions may assist decision-making, but may also lead to erroneous or problematic decisions.

Attention

- **Selective attention:** allows one to pay attention to a particular stimulus while determining if additional stimuli require attention in the background
- **Divided attention:** uses **automatic processing** to pay attention to multiple activities at one time

Language Areas in the Brain

- **Wernicke's area:** language comprehension; damage results in **Wernicke's aphasia** (fluent, nonsensical aphasia with lack of comprehension)
- **Broca's area:** motor function of speech; damage results in **Broca's aphasia** (nonfluent aphasia in which generating each word requires great effort)
- **Arcuate fasciculus:** connects Wernicke's and Broca's areas; damage results in **conduction aphasia** (the inability to repeat words despite intact speech generation and comprehension)

MOTIVATION, EMOTION, AND STRESS

Motivation

Motivation is the purpose or driving force behind our actions.

- **Extrinsic:** based on external circumstances
- **Intrinsic:** based on internal drive or perception

Motivation theories

- **Instinct theory:** innate, fixed patterns of behavior in response to stimuli
- **Arousal theory:** the state of being awake and reactive to stimuli; aim for optimal level of arousal for a given task (Yerkes–Dodson law)

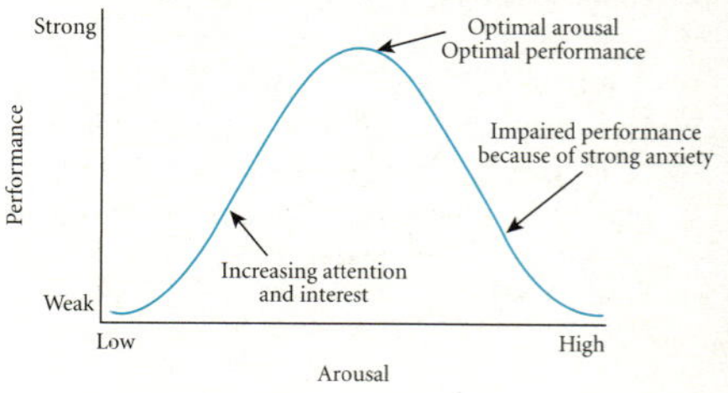

- **Drive reduction theory:** individuals act to relieve internal states of tension
- **Maslow's hierarchy of needs:** prioritizes needs into five categories: physiological needs (highest priority), safety and security, love and belonging, self-esteem, and self-actualization (lowest priority)

Emotion

Seven universal emotions: happiness, sadness, contempt, surprise, fear, disgust, anger

Theories of emotion:

Theory		First response	Second response
James–Lange		Nervous system arousal	Conscious emotion
Cannon–Bard	STIMULUS	Nervous system arousal and conscious emotion	Action
Schachter–Singer		Nervous system arousal and cognitive appraisal	Conscious emotion

Stress

Stress: the physiological and cognitive response to challenges or life changes

- **Primary appraisal:** classifying a potential stressor as irrelevant, benign–positive, or stressful
- **Secondary appraisal:** directed at evaluating whether the organism can cope with the stress, based on harm, threat, and challenge

Stressor (distress or eustress): anything that leads to a stress response; can include environmental, social, psychological, chemical, and biological stressors

The three stages of the **general adaptation syndrome** are alarm, resistance, and exhaustion.

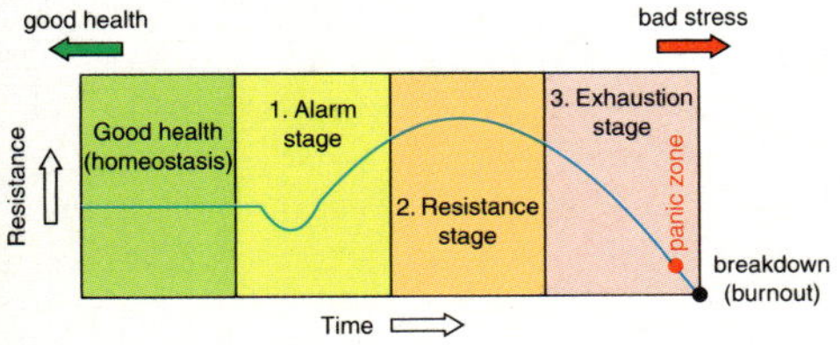

IDENTITY AND PERSONALITY

Self-Concept and Identity

- **Self-concept:** the sum of the ways in which we describe ourselves: in the present, who we used to be, and who we might be in the future
- **Identities:** individual components of our self-concept related to the groups to which we belong
- **Self-esteem:** our evaluation of ourselves
- **Self-efficacy:** the degree to which we see ourselves as being capable of a given skill in a given situation
- **Locus of control:** a self-evaluation that refers to the way we characterize the influences in our lives. Either **internal** (success or failure is a result of our own actions) or **external** (success or failure is a result of outside factors)

PSYCHOLOGICAL DISORDERS

***Diagnostic and Statistical Manual of Mental Disorders* (DSM):** the guide by which most psychological disorders are characterized, described, and diagnosed.

Schizophrenia and psychotic disorders

Schizophrenia: psychotic disorder characterized by distortions of reality and disturbances in content and form of thought, perception, and behavior. **Positive symptoms** include hallucinations, delusions, and disorganized thought and behavior. **Negative symptoms** include disturbance of affect and avolition.

Depressive disorders

- **Major depressive disorder:** contains at least one major depressive episode
- **Persistent depressive disorder:** a depressed mood (either **dysthymia** or major depression) for at least two years
- **Seasonal affective disorder:** the colloquial name for major depressive disorder with seasonal onset, with depression occurring during winter months

Bipolar and related disorders

- **Bipolar I disorder:** contains at least one manic episode
- **Bipolar II disorder:** contains at least one hypomanic episode and at least one major depressive episode
- **Cyclothymic disorder:** contains hypomanic episodes with dysthymia

Anxiety disorders

- **Generalized anxiety disorder:** constant disproportionate and persistent worry
- **Specific phobias:** irrational fears of specific objects
- **Social anxiety disorder:** anxiety due to social or performance situations
- **Agoraphobia:** fear of places or situations where it is hard for an individual to escape
- **Panic disorder:** recurrent attacks of intense, overwhelming fear and sympathetic nervous system activity with no clear stimulus. It may lead to **agoraphobia**.

Obsessive–compulsive disorder: obsessions (persistent, intrusive thoughts and impulses) and **compulsions** (repetitive tasks that relieve tension but cause significant impairment)

Body dysmorphic disorder: unrealistic negative evaluation of one's appearance or a specific body part

Dissociative disorders

- **Dissociative amnesia:** inability to recall past experience. May involve **dissociative fugue,** a sudden change in location that can involve the assumption of a new identity
- **Dissociative identity disorder:** two or more personalities that take control of behavior
- **Depersonalization/derealization disorder:** feelings of detachment from the mind and body, or from the environment

Formation of Identity

Freud's stages of psychosexual development

- Based on tensions caused by the **libido**, with failure at any given stage leading to **fixation**

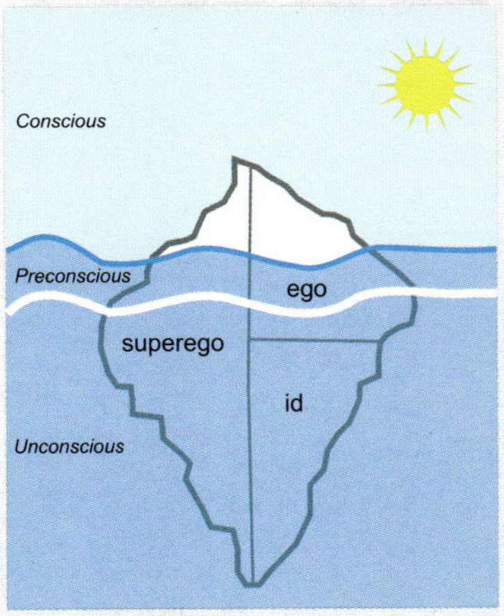

Erikson's stages of psychosocial development

- Stem from conflicts that are the result of decisions we are forced to make about ourselves and the environment around us at each phase of our lives
- Stages are trust *vs.* mistrust, autonomy *vs.* shame and doubt, initiative *vs.* guilt, industry *vs.* inferiority, identity *vs.* role confusion, intimacy *vs.* isolation, generativity *vs.* stagnation, integrity *vs.* despair

Kohlberg's theory of moral reasoning development

- Describes the approaches of individuals to resolving moral dilemmas
- Six stages are divided into three main phases: **preconventional**, **conventional**, and **postconventional**

Vygotsky's theory of cultural and biosocial development

- Describes development of language, culture, and skills

Personality

Psychoanalytic perspective: personality results from unconscious urges and desires

- Freud: id, superego, ego
- Jung: collective unconscious, archetypes

Humanistic perspective: emphasizes internal feelings of healthy individuals as they strive toward happiness and self-realization

- Maslow: hierarchy of needs
- Rogers: unconditional positive regard

Type and trait theory: personality can be described as a number of identifiable traits that carry characteristic behaviors

- Type theories of personality: ancient Greek humors, Sheldon's **somatotypes**, division into **Types A** and **B**, and the **Myers–Briggs Type Inventory**
- Eysenck's three major traits: psychoticism, extraversion, neuroticism
- Trait theorists' Big Five: openness, conscientiousness, extraversion, agreeableness, and neuroticism (OCEAN)
- Allport's three basic types of traits: cardinal, central, and secondary

Myers–Briggs Type Inventory

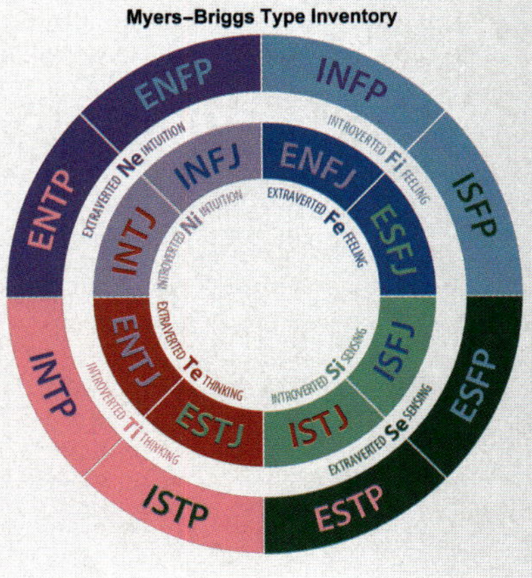

Somatic symptom and related disorders

- **Somatic symptom disorder:** at least one somatic symptom, which may or may not be linked to an underlying medical condition, that causes disproportionate concern
- **Illness anxiety disorder:** preoccupation with having or coming down with a serious medical condition
- **Conversion disorder:** unexplained symptoms affecting motor or sensory function

Personality disorders

Patterns of inflexible, maladaptive behavior that cause distress or impaired functioning

- **Cluster A** (odd, eccentric): paranoid, schizotypal, schizoid
- **Cluster B** (dramatic, emotional, erratic, "wild"): antisocial, borderline, histrionic, narcissistic
- **Cluster C** (anxious, fearful, "worried"): avoidant, dependent, obsessive–compulsive

SOCIAL PROCESSES, ATTITUDES, AND BEHAVIOR

Group Psychology

- **Social facilitation:** tendency to perform at a different level (better or worse) when others are around
- **Deindividuation:** loss of self-awareness in large groups; can lead to drastic changes in behavior
- **Bystander effect:** in a group, individuals are less likely to respond to a person in need
- **Peer pressure:** social influence placed on an individual by other individuals they consider equals
- **Group polarization:** tendency towards making decisions in a group that are more extreme than the thoughts of the individual group members
- **Groupthink:** tendency to make decisions based on ideas and solutions that arise within the group without considering outside ideas

Culture

- **Assimilation:** one culture begins to melt into another
- **Multiculturalism:** encouragement of multiple cultures within a community to enhance diversity
- **Subculture:** a group that distinguishes itself from the primary culture to which it belongs

Socialization

- **Socialization:** the process of developing and spreading norms, customs, and beliefs
- **Norms:** boundaries of acceptable behavior within society
- **Stigma:** extreme disapproval or dislike of a person or group based on perceived differences
- **Deviance:** any violation of norms, rules, or expectations within a society
- **Conformity:** changing beliefs or behaviors in order to fit into a group or society
- **Compliance:** individuals change behavior based on the request of others; techniques for gaining compliance include **foot-in-the-door, door-in-the-face, lowball,** and **that's-not-all**
- **Obedience:** change in behavior based on a command from someone seen as an authority figure

SOCIAL INTERACTION

Elements of Social Interaction

- **Status:** a position in society used to classify individuals. Can be **ascribed** (involuntarily assigned), **achieved** (voluntarily earned), or **master** (primary identity)
- **Role:** set of beliefs, values, and norms that define the expectations of a certain status
- **Group:** two or more individuals with similar characteristics who share a sense of unity
- **Network:** observable pattern of social relationships between individuals or groups
- **Organization:** group with a structure and culture designed to achieve specific goals; exists outside of each individual's membership within the organization

Self-Presentation and Interacting with Others

- **Display rules:** unspoken rules that govern the expression of emotion
- **Impression management:** maintenance of a public image through various strategies
- **Dramaturgical approach:** individuals create images of themselves in the same way that actors perform a role in front of an audience

SOCIAL THINKING

Social Behavior

- **Interpersonal attraction:** influenced by physical, social, and psychological factors
- **Aggression:** behavior with the intention to cause harm or increase social dominance
- **Attachment:** an emotional bond to another person; usually refers to the bond between a child and a caregiver
- **Altruism:** helping behavior in which the person's intent is to benefit someone else at a personal cost

SOCIAL PERCEPTION AND BEHAVIOR

Attribution Theory

Focuses on the tendency for individuals to infer the causes of other people's behavior

- **Dispositional (internal)** causes relate to the features of the person who is being considered
- **Situational (external)** causes relate to features of the surroundings or social context
- **Correspondent inference theory:** describes attributions made by observing the intentional (especially unexpected) behaviors performed by another person
- **Fundamental attribution error:** bias toward making dispositional attributions rather than situational attributions

Stereotypes, Prejudice, and Discrimination

- **Stereotypes:** attitudes and impressions that are made based on limited and superficial information
- **Self-fulfilling prophecy:** the phenomenon of a stereotype creating an expectation of a particular group, which creates conditions that lead to confirmation of this stereotype
- **Stereotype threat:** a feeling of anxiety about confirming a negative stereotype
- **Prejudice:** an irrationally based attitude prior to actual experience
- **Ethnocentrism:** the practice of making judgments about other cultures based on the values and beliefs of one's own culture (**in-group** *vs.* **out-group**)
- **Cultural relativism:** studying social groups and cultures on their own terms
- **Discrimination:** when prejudicial attitudes cause differences in treatment of a group

SOCIAL STRUCTURE AND DEMOGRAPHICS

Sociology: Theories and Institutions

- **Functionalism:** focuses on the function and relationships of each component of society
- **Conflict theory:** focuses on how power differentials are created and how they maintain order
- **Symbolic interactionism:** the study of how individuals interact through a shared understanding of words, gestures, and other symbols
- **Social constructionism:** explores how individuals and groups make decisions to agree upon a given social reality

Culture

- **Material culture:** physical items one associates with a given group (art, clothing, foods, buildings)
- **Symbolic culture:** the ideas associated with a cultural group

Demographics

Demographics: the statistical arm of sociology

Migration refers to the movement of people into (immigration) or out of (emigration) a geographical location.

Demographic transition: a model used to represent drops in birth and death rates as a result of industrialization

SOCIAL STRATIFICATION

Social Class

Social stratification is based on **socioeconomic status (SES)**.

- **Class:** a category of people with shared socioeconomic characteristics
- **Power:** the capacity to influence people through real or perceived rewards and punishments
- **Social capital:** the investment people make in society in return for economic or collective rewards
- **Social reproduction:** the passing on of social inequality, especially poverty, to other generations
- **Poverty:** low SES; in the US, the poverty line is the government's calculation of the minimum income requirements to acquire the minimum necessities of life

Epidemiology

Incidence: $\frac{\text{new cases}}{\text{population at risk}}$ per time

Prevalence: $\frac{\text{number of cases (new or old)}}{\text{total population}}$ per time

Morbidity: the burden or degree of illness associated with a given disease

Mortality: deaths caused by a given disease

AMINO ACIDS, PEPTIDES, AND PROTEINS

Amino Acids Found in Proteins

Amino acids have an amino group, carboxylic acid, a hydrogen atom, and an **R group** attached to a central α-carbon.

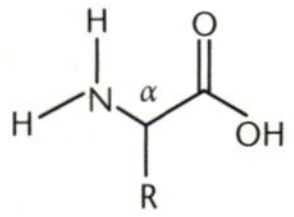

Amino acids are chiral (L), except for glycine; and have the (*S*) configuration, except for cysteine.

Side chains determine the chemistry and function of amino acids.

Nonpolar, Nonaromatic

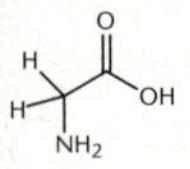
glycine (Gly, G)

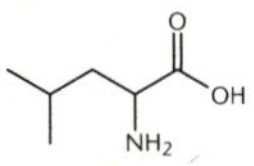
leucine (Leu, L)

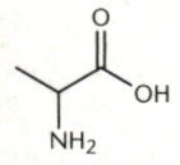
alanine (Ala, A)

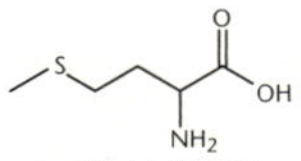
methionine (Met, M)

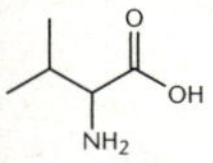
valine (Val, V)

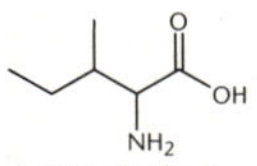
isoleucine (Ile, I)

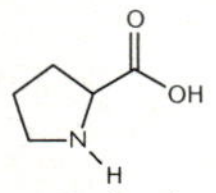
proline (Pro, P)

Positively Charged

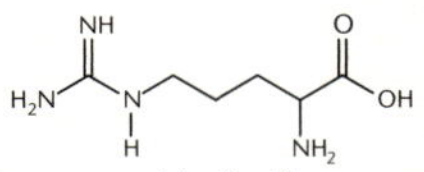
arginine (Arg, R)

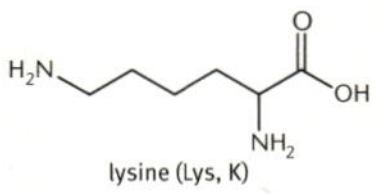
lysine (Lys, K)

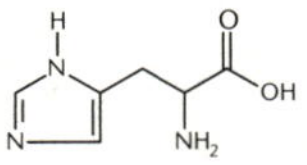
histidine (His, H)

Acid–Base Chemistry of Amino Acids

Amino acids are amphoteric.

- At low (acidic) pH: fully protonated
- At neutral pH: zwitterion
- At high (basic) pH: fully deprotonated

pI is determined by averaging the pK_a values that refer to protonation and deprotonation of the zwitterion.

Negatively Charged

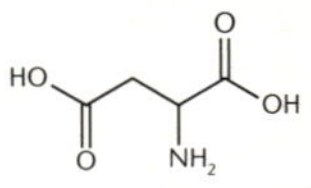
aspartic acid (Asp, D)

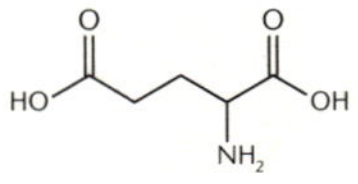
glutamic acid (Glu, E)

Polar

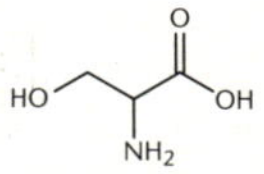
serine (Ser, S)

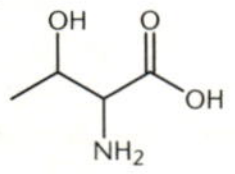
threonine (Thr, T)

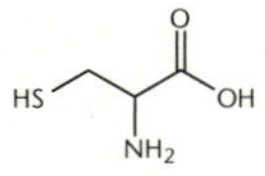
cysteine (Cys, C)

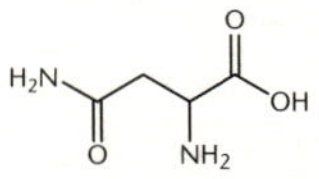
asparagine (Asn, N)

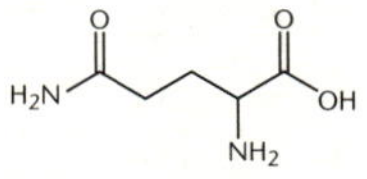
glutamine (Gln, Q)

Aromatic Side Chains

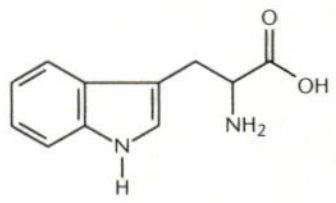
tryptophan (Trp, W)

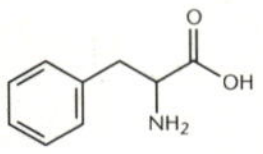
phenylalanine (Phe, F)

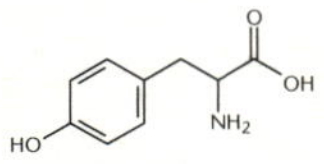
tyrosine (Tyr, Y)

Peptide Bond Formation and Hydrolysis

Peptide bond formation is a **condensation** (**dehydration**) reaction with a nucleophilic amino group attacking an electrophilic carbonyl. Peptide bonds are broken by **hydrolysis**.

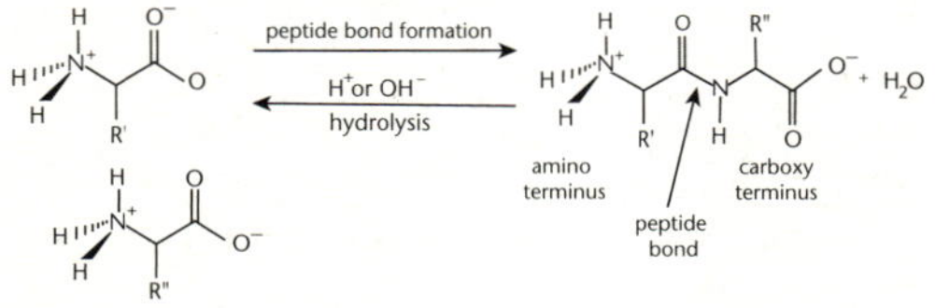

Protein Structure

Primary structure: linear sequence of amino acids

Secondary structure: local structure, stabilized by hydrogen bonding

- α-helices
- β-pleated sheets

Tertiary structure: three-dimensional structure stabilized by hydrophobic interactions, acid–base interactions (salt bridges), hydrogen bonding, and disulfide bonds

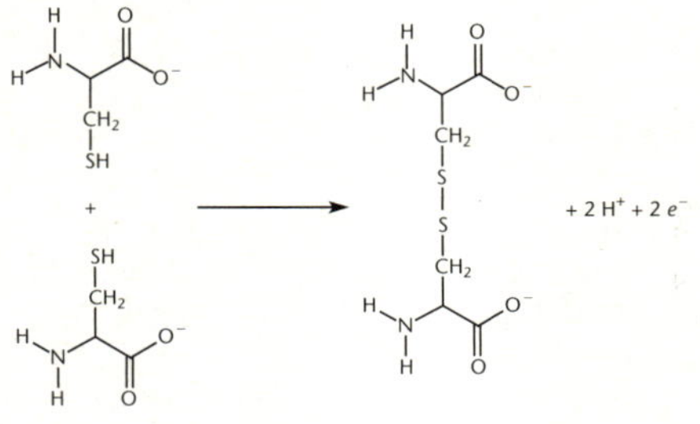

cysteine cystine

Quaternary structure: interactions between subunits

Heat and solutes can cause **denaturation**.

ENZYMES

Enzymes, like all catalysts, lower the activation energy necessary for reactions. They do not alter the free energy (ΔG) or enthalpy (ΔH) change that accompanies the reaction nor the final equilibrium position; rather, they change the rate (kinetics) at which equilibrium is reached.

- **Ligases** are responsible for joining two large biomolecules, often of the same type.
- **Isomerases** catalyze the interconversion of isomers, including both constitutional and stereoisomers.
- **Lyases** catalyze cleavage without the addition of water and without the transfer of electrons. The reverse reaction (synthesis) is usually more biologically important.
- **Hydrolases** catalyze cleavage with the addition of water.
- **Oxidoreductases** catalyze oxidation–reduction reactions that involve the transfer of electrons.
- **Transferases** move a functional group from one molecule to another molecule.

Michaelis–Menten

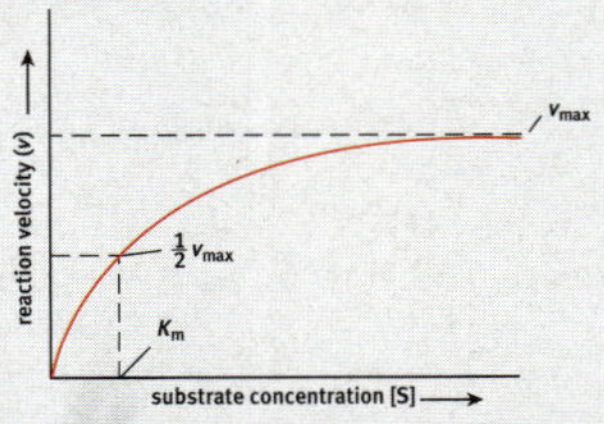

Cooperative enzymes show a **sigmoidal** curve.

Lineweaver–Burk

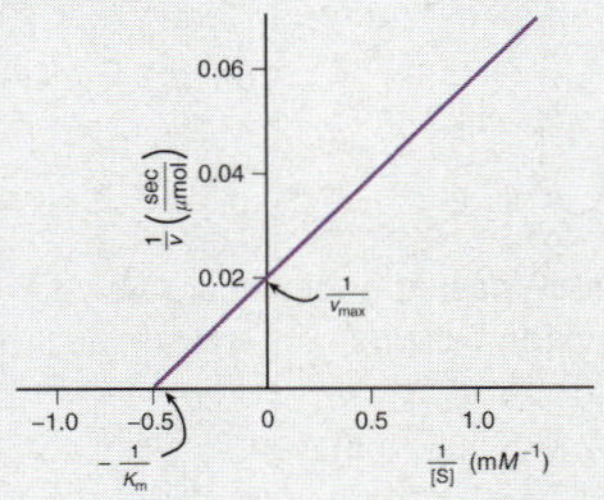

Enzyme Kinetics

Saturation kinetics: As substrate concentration increases, the reaction rate also increases until a maximum value is reached.

$$v = \frac{v_{max}[S]}{K_m + [S]}$$

At one-half v_{max}, $[S] = K_m$

Regulation of Enzyme Activity

	Competitive	Noncompetitive	Mixed	Uncompetitive
Binding Site	Active site	Allosteric site	Allosteric site	Enzyme-substrate complex
Impact on K_m	Increases	No change	Increases or Decreases	Decreases
Impact on v_{max}	No change	Decreases	Decreases	Decreases

NONENZYMATIC PROTEIN FUNCTION AND PROTEIN ANALYSIS

Cellular Functions

Structural proteins: generally fibrous. Include **collagen, elastin, keratin, actin,** and **tubulin**

Motor proteins: capable of force generation through a conformational change. Include **myosin, kinesin,** and **dynein**

Binding proteins: bind a specific substrate, either to sequester it in the body or hold its concentration at steady state

Cell adhesion molecules (CAM): bind cells to other cells or surfaces. Include **cadherins, integrins,** and **selectins**

Antibodies (**immunoglobulins, Ig**)**:** target a specific **antigen**, which may be a protein on the surface of a pathogen (invading organism) or a toxin

Biosignaling

Ion channels can be used for regulating ion flow into or out of a cell. There are three main types of ion channels: **ungated channels, voltage-gated channels,** and **ligand-gated channels.**

Enzyme-linked receptors participate in cell signaling through extracellular ligand binding and initiation of second messenger cascades.

G protein-coupled receptors have a membrane-bound protein associated with a trimeric **G protein.** They also initiate second messenger systems.

CARBOHYDRATE STRUCTURE AND FUNCTION

Carbohydrate Classification

Carbohydrates are organized by their number of carbon atoms and functional groups.

- 3-carbon sugars are **trioses,** 4-carbon sugars are **tetroses,** and so on.
- Sugars with aldehydes as their most oxidized group are **aldoses**; sugars with ketones as their most oxidized group are **ketoses**.

Sugars with the highest-numbered chiral carbon with the –OH group on the right (in a Fischer projection) are D-sugars; those with the –OH on the left are L-sugars. D- and L-forms of the same sugar are **enantiomers**.

Diastereomers differ at at least one—but not all—chiral carbons. Also include:

- **Epimers** differ at exactly one chiral carbon.
- **Anomers** are a subtype of epimers that differ at the anomeric carbon.

Cyclic Sugar Molecules

Cyclization describes the ring formation of carbohydrates from their straight-chain forms.

When rings form, the anomeric carbon can take on either an α- or β-conformation.

The **anomeric carbon** is the new chiral center formed in ring closure; it was the carbon containing the carbonyl in the straight-chain form.

- **α-anomers** have the –OH on the anomeric carbon *trans* to the free $-CH_2OH$ group.
- **β-anomers** have the –OH on the anomeric carbon *cis* to the free $-CH_2OH$ group.

During **mutarotation**, one anomeric form shifts to another, with the straight-chain form as an intermediate.

Monosaccharides

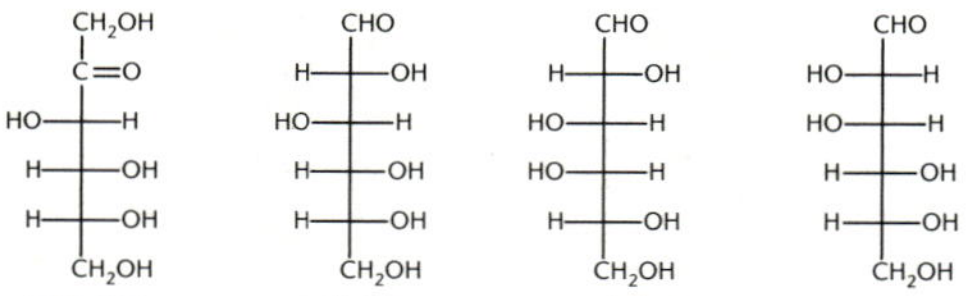

D-fructose D-glucose D-galactose D-mannose

Monosaccharides are single carbohydrate units and can undergo three main reactions: **oxidation–reduction**, **esterification**, and **glycoside formation**.

Glycoside formation is the basis for building complex carbohydrates and requires the anomeric carbon to link to another sugar.

Sugars with a –H replacing an –OH group are termed **deoxy sugars**.

Disaccharides

Common **disaccharides** include **sucrose** (glucose-α-1,2-fructose), **lactose** (galactose-β-1,4-glucose), and **maltose** (glucose-α-1,4-glucose).

Polysaccharides

- **Cellulose:** main structural component of plant cell walls; main source of fiber in the human diet
- **Starches (amylose and amylopectin):** main energy storage forms for plants
- **Glycogen:** a major energy storage form for animals

DNA AND BIOTECHNOLOGY

DNA Structure

Nucleosides contain a five-carbon sugar bonded to a nitrogenous base; **nucleotides** are nucleosides with one to three phosphate groups added. ATP is a high-energy nucleotide with an adenosine nucleoside.

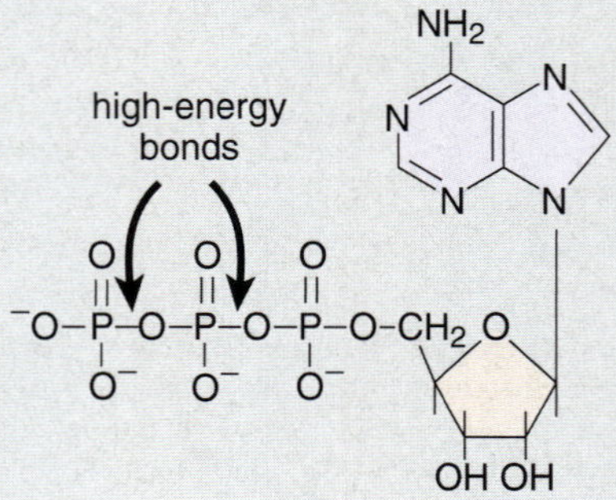

ATP

Nucleotides in DNA contain deoxyribose; in RNA, they contain ribose.

Nucleotides are abbreviated by letter: adenine (A), cytosine (C), guanine (G), thymine (T), and uracil (U).

Watson–Crick Model

- The DNA backbone is composed of alternating sugar and phosphate groups, and is always read **5'** to **3'**.
- There are two strands with **antiparallel** polarity, wound into a **double helix**.
- **Purines** (A and G) always pair with **pyrimidines** (C, U, and T). In DNA, A pairs with T (via two hydrogen bonds) and C pairs with G (via three hydrogen bonds). In RNA, A pairs with U (via two hydrogen bonds).
- **Chargaff's rules:** purines and pyrimidines are equal in number in a DNA molecule. The amount of A equals the amount of T, and the amount of C equals the amount of G.

DNA strands can be pulled apart (**denatured**) and brought back together (**reannealed**).

Eukaryotic Chromosome Organization

DNA is organized into 46 chromosomes in human cells.

In eukaryotes, DNA is wound around **histone proteins** (H2A, H2B, H3, and H4) to form **nucleosomes**, which may be stabilized by another histone protein (H1). DNA and its associated histones make up **chromatin** in the nucleus.

- **Heterochromatin** is dense, transcriptionally silent DNA.
- **Euchromatin** is less dense, transcriptionally active DNA.

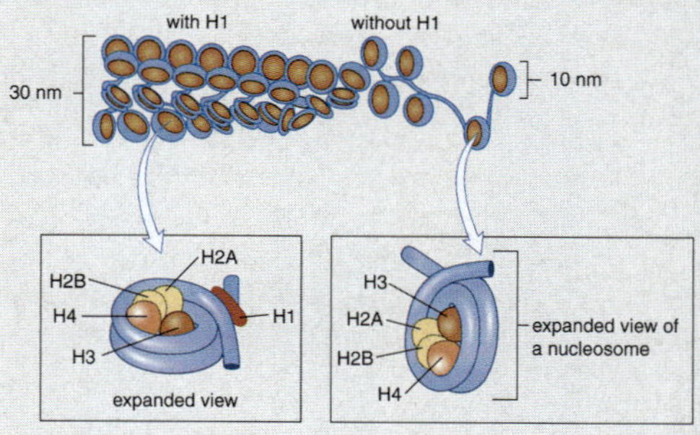

Telomeres are the ends of chromosomes. They contain high GC-content to prevent DNA unraveling.

Centromeres hold sister chromatids together until they are separated during anaphase in mitosis. They also contain a high GC-content.

DNA Replication

Step in Replication	Prokaryotic Cells	Eukaryotic Cells (Nuclei)
Origin of replication	One per chromosome	Multiple per chromosome
Unwinding of DNA double helix	Helicase	Helicase
Stabilization of unwound template strands	Single-stranded DNA-binding protein	Single-stranded DNA-binding protein
Synthesis of RNA primers	Primase	Primase
Synthesis of DNA	DNA polymerase III	DNA polymerases α, δ, and ε
Removal of RNA primers	DNA polymerase I (5′→3′ exonuclease)	RNase H (5′→3′ exonuclease)
Replacement of RNA with DNA	DNA polymerase I	DNA polymerase δ
Joining of Okazaki fragments	DNA ligase	DNA ligase
Removal of positive supercoils ahead of advancing replication forks	DNA topoisomerases (DNA gyrase)	DNA topoisomerases
Synthesis of telomeres	Not applicable	Telomerase

DNA replication is **semiconservative**: one old **parent strand** and one new **daughter strand** is incorporated into each of the two new DNA molecules.

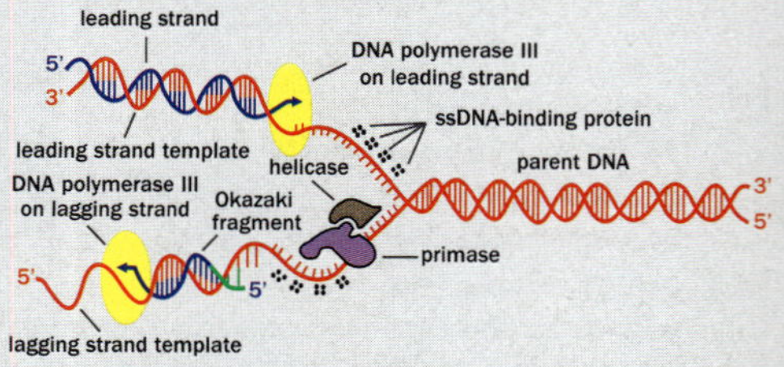

DNA polymerase synthesizes new DNA strands, reading the template DNA 3′ to 5′ and synthesizing the new strand 5′ to 3′.

- The **leading strand** requires only one primer and can then be synthesized continuously.
- The **lagging strand** requires many primers and is synthesized in discrete sections called **Okazaki fragments**.

Recombinant DNA and Biotechnology

Recombinant DNA is DNA composed of nucleotides from two different sources.

DNA cloning introduces a fragment of DNA into a **vector plasmid**. A **restriction enzyme** (**restriction endonuclease**) cuts both the plasmid and the fragment, leaving them with **sticky ends**, which can bind.

Once replicated, the bacterial cells can be used to create a protein of interest, or can be lysed to allow for isolation of the fragment of interest from the vector.

DNA libraries are large collections of known DNA sequences.

- **Genomic libraries** contain large fragments of DNA, including both coding and noncoding regions of the genome. They cannot be used to make recombinant proteins or for gene therapy.
- **cDNA libraries** (**expression libraries**) contain smaller fragments of DNA, and only include the exons of genes expressed by the sample tissue. They can be used to make recombinant proteins or for gene therapy.

Hybridization is the joining of complementary base pair sequences.

Polymerase chain reaction (**PCR**) is an automated process by which millions of copies of a DNA sequence can be created from a very small sample by hybridization.

DNA molecules can be separated by size using **agarose gel electrophoresis**.

Southern blotting can be used to detect the presence and quantity of various DNA strands in a sample. After electrophoresis, the sample is transferred to a membrane that can be **probed** with single-stranded DNA molecules to look for a sequence of interest.

DNA sequencing uses **dideoxyribonucleotides**, which terminate the DNA chain because they lack a 3′–OH group.

RNA AND THE GENETIC CODE

Central Dogma: DNA → RNA → proteins

The Genetic Code

Degenerate code allows multiple codons to encode for the same amino acid.

- **Initiation:** AUG (methionine)
- **Termination:** UAA, UGA, UAG
- Redundancy and **wobble** (third base in the codon) allow mutations to occur without affecting the protein.

Point mutations can cause:

- **Silent** mutations, with no effect on protein synthesis
- **Nonsense (truncation)** mutations, which produce a premature stop codon
- **Missense** mutations, which produce a codon that codes for a different amino acid
- **Frameshift mutations**, which result from nucleotide addition or deletion and change the reading frame of subsequent codons

RNA is structurally similar to DNA except:

- Substitution of a ribose sugar for deoxyribose
- Substitution of uracil for thymine
- Single-stranded instead of double-stranded

There are three major types of RNA in transcription:

- **Messenger RNA (mRNA):** carries the message from DNA in the nucleus via transcription of the gene; travels into the cytoplasm to be translated
- **Transfer RNA (tRNA):** brings in amino acids; recognizes the codon on the mRNA using its anticodon
- **Ribosomal RNA (rRNA):** makes up much of the ribosome; enzymatically active

Transcription

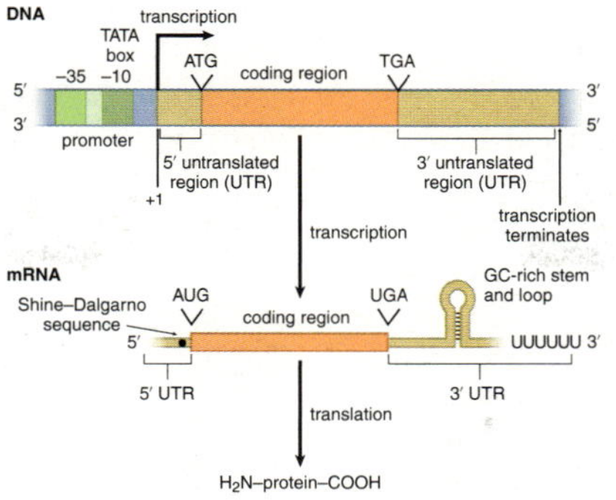

Steps:

- Helicase and topoisomerase unwind DNA double helix.
- **RNA polymerase II** binds to **TATA box** within **promoter** region of gene (25 base pairs upstream from first transcribed base).
- **hnRNA** synthesized from DNA template (antisense) strand.

Posttranscriptional modifications:

- 7-methylguanylate triphosphate cap added to 5′ end
- Polyadenosyl (poly-A) tail added to 3′ end
- Splicing done by **spliceosome**; introns removed and exons ligated together. **Alternative splicing** combines different exons to acquire different gene products.

Translation

Occurs at the ribosome.

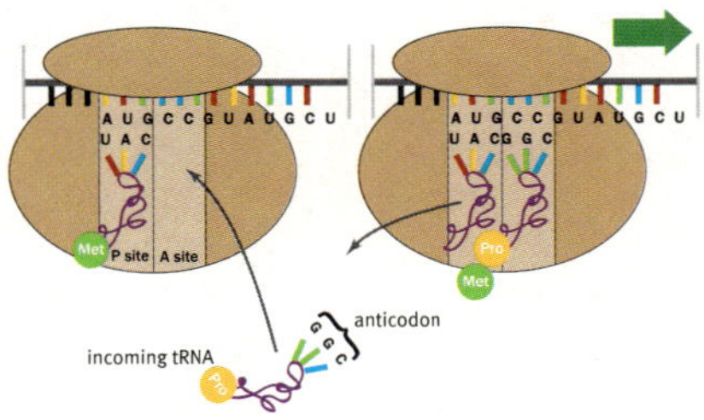

Three stages: **initiation**, **elongation**, **termination**

Posttranslational modifications:

- Folding by **chaperones**
- Formation of quaternary structure
- Cleavage of proteins or signal sequences
- Covalent addition of other biomolecules (phosphorylation, carboxylation, glycosylation, prenylation)

Control of Gene Expression in Prokaryotes

Operons (Jacob–Monod model) are inducible or repressible clusters of genes transcribed as a single mRNA.

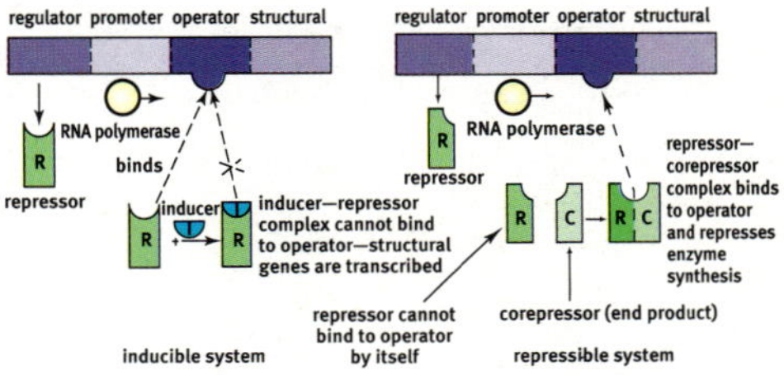

Control of Gene Expression in Eukaryotes

Transcription factors search for promoter and enhancer regions in the DNA.

- **Promoters** are within 25 base pairs of the transcription start site.
- **Enhancers** are more than 25 base pairs away from the transcription start site.

BIOLOGICAL MEMBRANES

Membrane Transport

Osmotic pressure, a **colligative property**, is the pressure applied to a pure solvent to prevent osmosis and is related to the concentration of the solution.

$$\Pi = iMRT$$

Passive transport does not require ATP because the molecule is moving down its concentration gradient or from an area of higher concentration to an area of lower concentration.

- **Simple diffusion** does not require a transporter. Small, nonpolar molecules passively move from an area of high concentration to an area of low concentration until equilibrium is achieved.
- **Osmosis** describes the diffusion of water across a selectively permeable membrane.
- **Facilitated diffusion** uses transport proteins to move impermeable solutes across the cell membrane.

Active transport requires energy in the form of ATP (**primary**) or an existing favorable ion gradient (**secondary**). Secondary active transport can be further classified as **symport** or **antiport**.

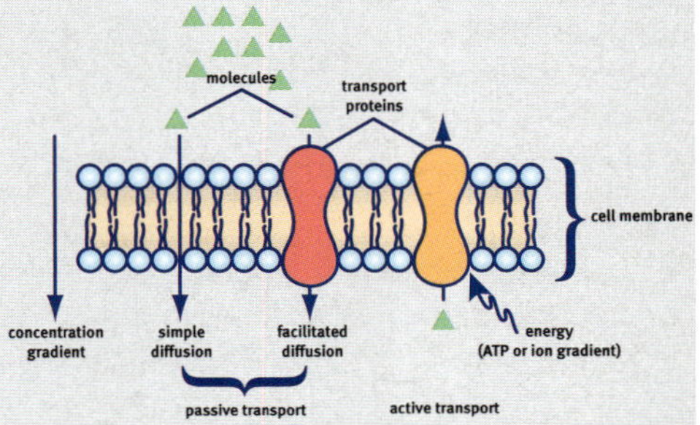

Endocytosis and **exocytosis** are methods of engulfing material into cells or releasing material to the exterior of cells, both via the cell membrane. **Pinocytosis** is the ingestion of liquid into the cell from vesicles formed from the cell membrane and **phagocytosis** is the ingestion of solid material.

CARBOHYDRATE METABOLISM

Glycolysis

Occurs in the cytoplasm of all cells, and does not require oxygen. Yields 2 ATP per glucose. Important enzymes include:

- **Glucokinase:** present in the pancreatic β-islet cells as part of the glucose sensor and is responsive to insulin in the liver
- **Hexokinase:** traps glucose
- **Phosphofructokinase-1** (**PFK-1**)**:** rate-limiting step
- **Phosphofructokinase-2** (**PFK-2**)**:** produces F2,6-BP, which activates PFK-1
- **Glyceraldehyde-3-phosphate dehydrogenase:** produces NADH
- **3-phosphoglycerate kinase** and **pyruvate kinase:** perform **substrate-level phosphorylation**

Glucokinase/hexokinase, PFK-1, and pyruvate kinase catalyze irreversible reactions.

The NADH produced in glycolysis is oxidized aerobically by the mitochondrial electron transport chain and anaerobically by cytoplasmic **lactate dehydrogenase**.

Pyruvate Dehydrogenase

- Converts pyruvate to acetyl-CoA. Stimulated by insulin and inhibited by acetyl-CoA.

The Citric Acid Cycle

Takes place in mitochondrial matrix. Main purpose is to oxidize acetyl-CoA to CO_2 and generate high-energy electron carriers (NADH and $FADH_2$) and GTP.

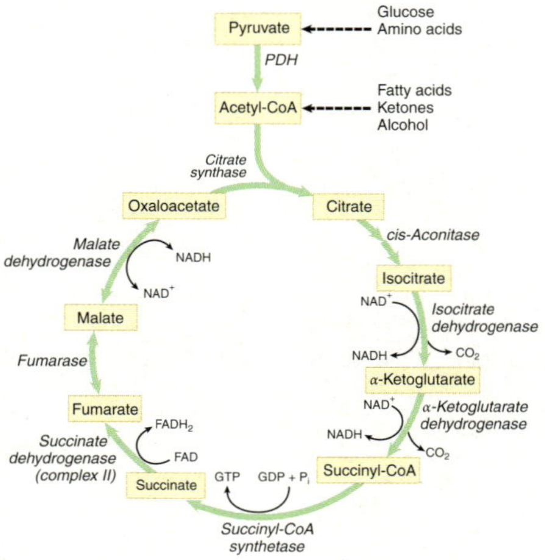

The Electron Transport Chain

Takes place on the matrix-facing surface of the inner mitochondrial membrane.

NADH donates electrons to the chain, which are passed from one complex to the next. Reduction potentials increase down the chain, until the electrons end up on oxygen, which has the highest reduction potential.

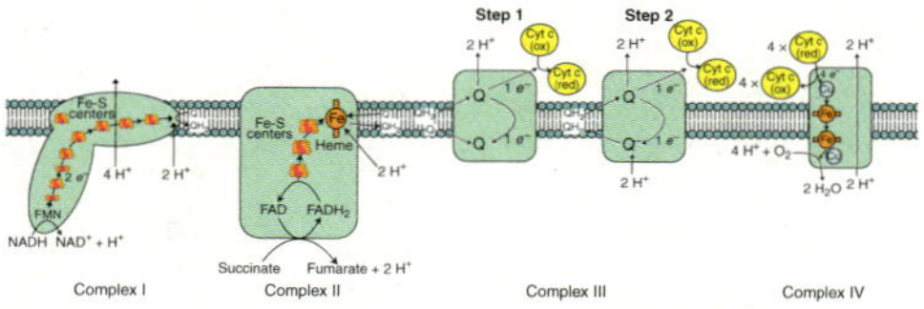

NADH cannot cross the inner mitochondrial membrane, so must use one of two shuttle mechanisms to transfer its electrons to energy carriers in the mitochondrial matrix: the **glycerol 3-phosphate shuttle** or the **malate–aspartate shuttle**.

Oxidative Phosphorylation

The **proton-motive force** is the electrochemical gradient generated by the electron transport chain across the inner mitochondrial membrane. The intermembrane space has a higher concentration of protons than the matrix; this gradient stores energy, which can be used to form ATP via **chemiosmotic coupling**.

ATP synthase is the enzyme responsible for generating ATP from ADP and an inorganic phosphate (P_i).

Summary of the energy yield of the various carbohydrate metabolism processes:

- Glycolysis: 2 NADH and 2 ATP
- Pyruvate dehydrogenase: 1 NADH (2 NADH per molecule of glucose because each glucose forms two molecules of pyruvate)
- Citric acid cycle: 3 NADH, 1 $FADH_2$, and 1 GTP (6 NADH, 2 $FADH_2$, and 2 GTP per molecule of glucose)
- Each NADH: 2.5 ATP; 10 NADH form 25 ATP
- Each $FADH_2$: 1.5 ATP; 2 $FADH_2$ form 3 ATP
- GTP are converted to ATP.
- 2 ATP from glycolysis + 2 ATP (GTP) from citric acid cycle + 25 ATP from NADH + 3 ATP from $FADH_2$ = 32 ATP per molecule of glucose (optimal). 30–32 ATP per molecule of glucose is the commonly accepted range for energy yield.

Glycogenesis and Glycogenolysis

Glycogenesis (glycogen synthesis) is the building of glycogen using two main enzymes:

- **Glycogen synthase**, which creates α-1,4 glycosidic links between glucose molecules. It is activated by insulin in the liver and muscles.
- **Branching enzyme**, which moves a block of oligoglucose from one chain and connects it as a branch using an α-1,6 glycosidic link.

Glycogenolysis is the breakdown of glycogen using two main enzymes:

- **Glycogen phosphorylase**, which removes single glucose 1-phosphate molecules by breaking α-1,4 glycosidic links. In the liver, it is activated by glucagon to prevent low blood sugar. In exercising skeletal muscle, it is activated by epinephrine and AMP to provide glucose for the muscle itself.
- **Debranching enzyme**, which moves a block of oligoglucose from one branch and connects it to the chain using an α-1,4 glycosidic link.

Gluconeogenesis

Occurs in both the cytoplasm and mitochondria, predominantly in the liver. Most of gluconeogenesis is just the reverse of glycolysis, using the same enzymes.

The three irreversible steps of glycolysis must be bypassed by different enzymes:

- Pyruvate carboxylase and PEP carboxykinase bypass pyruvate kinase
- Fructose-1,6-bisphosphatase bypasses phosphofructokinase-1
- Glucose-6-phosphatase bypasses hexokinase/ glucokinase

The Pentose Phosphate Pathway

Occurs in the cytoplasm of most cells, generating **NADPH** and sugars for biosynthesis. Rate-limiting enzyme is **glucose-6-phosphate dehydrogenase**, which is activated by $NADP^+$ and insulin and inhibited by NADPH.

BIOENERGETICS AND REGULATION OF METABOLISM

Metabolic States

- In the **postprandial/well-fed (absorptive) state**, insulin secretion is high and anabolic metabolism prevails.
- In the **postabsorptive (fasting) state**, insulin secretion decreases while glucagon and catecholamine secretion increases.
- Prolonged fasting (**starvation**) dramatically increases glucagon and catecholamine secretion. Most tissues rely on fatty acids.

LIPID AND AMINO ACID METABOLISM

Lipid Transport

Lipids are transported via **chylomicrons**, **VLDL**, **IDL**, **LDL**, and **HDL**.

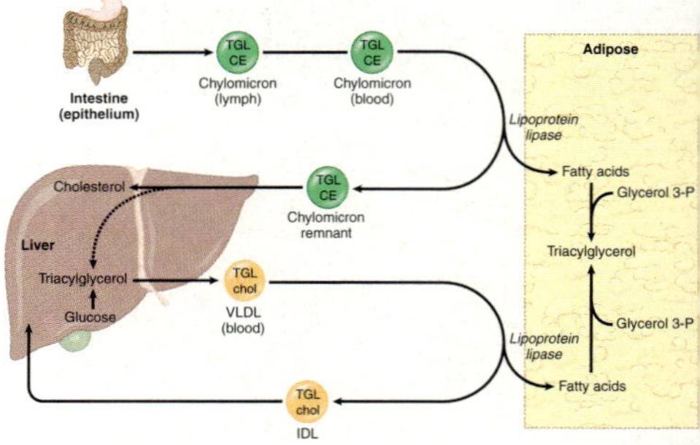

Cholesterol Metabolism

- Cholesterol may be obtained through dietary sources or through synthesis in the liver.
- The key enzyme in cholesterol biosynthesis is **HMG-CoA reductase**.

Palmitic acid, the only fatty acid that humans can synthesize, is produced in the cytoplasm from acetyl-CoA transported out of the mitochondria.

Fatty acid oxidation occurs in the mitochondria, following transport by the carnitine shuttle, via **β-oxidation**.

Ketone bodies form (**ketogenesis**) during a prolonged starvation state due to excess acetyl-CoA in the liver. **Ketolysis** regenerates acetyl-CoA for use as an energy source in peripheral tissues.

Protein Catabolism

Protein digestion occurs primarily in the small intestine. Carbon skeletons of amino acids are used for energy, either through gluconeogenesis or ketone body formation. Amino groups are fed into the **urea cycle** for excretion.

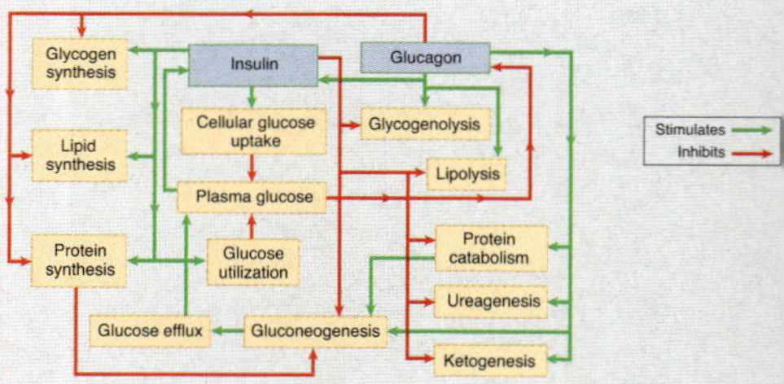

Tissue-Specific Metabolism

- Liver: maintains blood glucose through glycogenolysis and gluconeogenesis. Processes lipids, cholesterol, bile, urea, and toxins.
- Adipose: stores and releases lipids
- Resting muscle: conserves carbohydrates as glycogen and uses free fatty acids for fuel
- Active muscle: may use anaerobic metabolism, oxidative phosphorylation, direct phosphorylation (creatine phosphate), or fatty acid oxidation
- Cardiac muscle: uses fatty acid oxidation
- Brain: uses glucose except in prolonged starvation, when it can use ketolysis

THE CELL

Organelles of Eukaryotic Cells

- **Nucleus:** contains all of the genetic material necessary for replication of the cell
- **Mitochondrion:** location of many metabolic processes (pyruvate dehydrogenase, citric acid cycle, ETC, oxidative phosphorylation, β-oxidation, some of gluconeogenesis, urea cycle) and ATP production
- **Lysosomes:** membrane-bound structures containing hydrolytic enzymes capable of breaking down many different substrates
- **Rough endoplasmic reticulum:** interconnected membranous structure with ribosomes studding the outside; site of synthesis of proteins destined for insertion into a membrane or secretion
- **Smooth endoplasmic reticulum:** interconnected membranous structure where lipid synthesis and detoxification occurs
- **Golgi apparatus:** membrane-bound sacs where posttranslational modification of proteins occurs
- **Peroxisomes:** organelle containing hydrogen peroxide; site of β-oxidation of very long chain fatty acids

Fluid Mosaic Model and Membrane Traffic

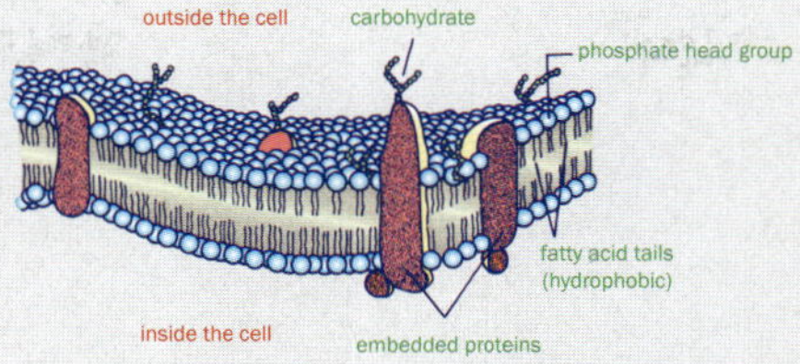

- Phospholipid bilayer with cholesterol and embedded proteins
- Exterior: hydrophilic phosphate head groups
- Interior: hydrophobic fatty acids

The original form of the **cell theory** consisted of three basic tenets:

- All living things are composed of cells.
- The cell is the basic functional unit of life.
- Cells arise only from preexisting cells.

A fourth tenet has been added as a result of advances in molecular biology: cells carry genetic information in the form of DNA. This genetic material is passed on from parent to daughter cell.

Eukaryotes contain membrane-bound organelles such as a nucleus, while prokaryotes are simpler cells without a nucleus.

Prokaryotes

- Classified by shape: Spherical bacteria are known as **cocci**, while rod-shaped bacteria are known as **bacilli**. Spiral-shaped bacteria are known as **spirilli**.
- Cell wall and cell membrane form the envelope. Composition of the cell wall further classifies bacteria into gram-positive and gram-negative. **Gram-positive** bacteria have large quantities of peptidoglycan in the cell wall, while **gram-negative** bacteria have much smaller quantities of peptidoglycan with lipopolysaccharides.
- Structure of flagella in bacteria is much different than that of eukaryotes. Eukaryotic flagella contain a basal body that serves as the engine for motion.
- All prokaryotes divide by **binary fission**. The circular chromosome replicates and attaches to the cell wall; the plasma membrane and cell wall grow along the midline, forming daughter cells.

REPRODUCTION

Cell Division

- G_1: cell increases its organelles and cytoplasm
- S: DNA replication
- G_2: same as G_1
- M: the cell divides in two
- Mitosis = PMAT
- Meiosis = PMAT × 2

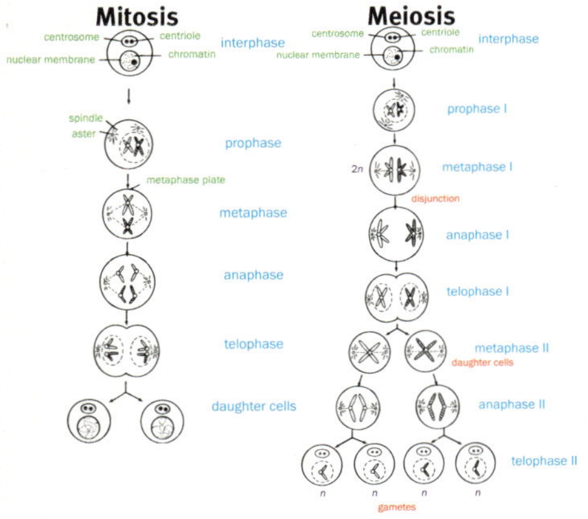

Sexual Reproduction

Meiosis I:

- Two pairs of sister chromatids form tetrads during prophase I.
- Crossing over leads to genetic recombination in prophase I.
- Homologous chromosomes separate during metaphase I.

Meiosis II:

- Essentially identical to mitosis, but no replication.
- Meiosis occurs in **spermatogenesis** (sperm formation) and **oogenesis** (egg formation).

Four Stages of Early Development

Cleavage: mitotic divisions

Implantation: embryo implants during blastula stage

Gastrulation: ectoderm, endoderm, and mesoderm form

Neurulation: germ layers develop a nervous system

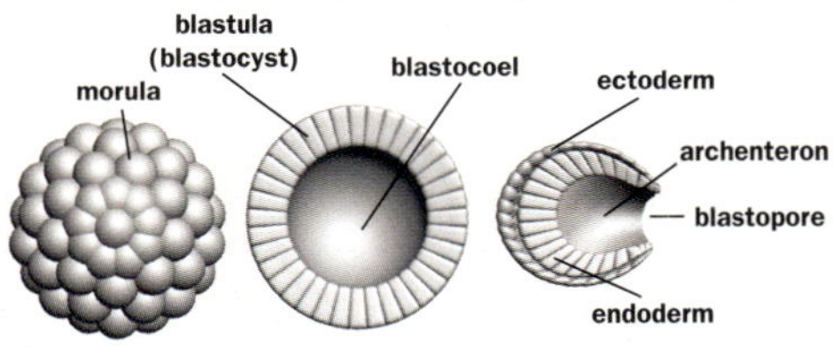

Ectoderm "Attract"oderm	Nervous system, epidermis, lens of eye, inner ear
Endoderm "Endernal" organs	Lining of digestive tract, lungs, liver and pancreas
Mesoderm "Means"oderm	Muscles, skeleton, circulatory system, gonads, kidney

The Liver's Roles in Homeostasis

1. Gluconeogenesis
2. Processing of nitrogenous wastes (urea)
3. Detoxification of wastes/chemicals/drugs
4. Storage of iron and vitamin A
5. Synthesis of bile and blood proteins
6. β-Oxidation of fatty acids to ketones
7. Interconversion of carbohydrates, fats, and amino acids

Layers of the Skin

- Stratum corneum
- Stratum lucidum
- Stratum granulosum
- Stratum spinosum
- Stratum basalis

HOMEOSTASIS

Osmoregulation

- **Filtration** at the glomerulus. Filtrate (fluid and small solutes) passes through. *Passive*
- **Secretion** of acids, bases, and ions from interstitial fluid to filtrate. Maintains pH, [K^+] and [waste]. *Passive and Active*
- **Reabsorption:** essential substances and water flow from filtrate to blood. Enabled by osmolarity gradient and selective permeability of the walls. *Passive and Active*

Hormonal Regulation

Aldosterone

- Stimulates Na^+ reabsorption, K^+ and H^+ secretion, increasing water reabsorption, blood volume, and blood pressure
- Secreted from adrenal cortex
- Is regulated by the renin–angiotensin–aldosterone system

ADH (Vasopressin)

Increases collecting duct's permeability to water to increase water reabsorption

- Is secreted from posterior pituitary with high [solute] in the blood

Kidneys regulate [salt] and [water] in the blood. Their functional unit is the nephron.

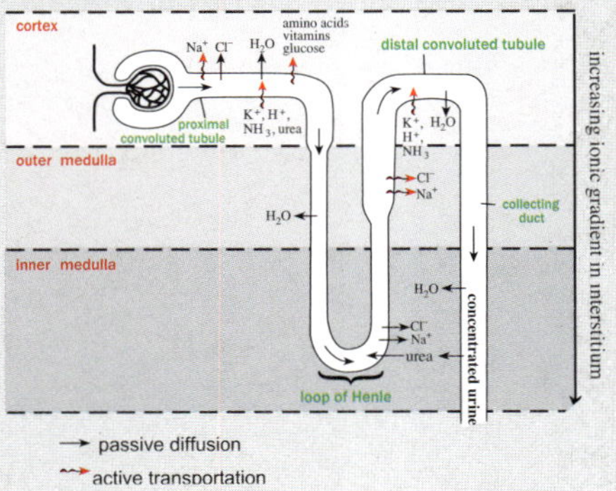

ENDOCRINE SYSTEM

Direct hormones directly stimulate organs; tropic hormones stimulate other glands.
Mechanisms of hormone action: **peptides** act via second messengers and **steroids** act via hormone/receptor binding to DNA. Amino acid-derivative hormones may do either.

Hormone	Source	Action
Follicle-stimulating (FSH)	Anterior pituitary	Stimulates follicle maturation; spermatogenesis
Luteinizing (LH)		Stimulates ovulation; testosterone synthesis
Adrenocorticotropic (ACTH)		Stimulates adrenal cortex to make and secrete glucocorticoids
Thyroid-stimulating (TSH)		Stimulates the thyroid to produce thyroid hormones
Prolactin		Stimulates milk production and secretion
Endorphins		Inhibits the perception of pain in the brain
Growth hormone		Stimulates bone and muscle growth/lipolysis
Oxytocin	Hypothalamus; stored in posterior pituitary	Stimulates uterine contractions during labor, milk secretion during lactation
Antidiuretic (ADH, vasopressin)		Stimulates water reabsorption in kidneys
Thyroid hormones (T_3, T_4)	Thyroid	Stimulates metabolic activity
Calcitonin		Decreases (tones down) blood calcium level
Parathyroid hormone	Parathyroid	Increases blood calcium level
Glucocorticoids	Adrenal cortex	Increases blood glucose level and decreases protein synthesis; anti-inflammatory
Mineralocorticoids		Increases sodium and water reabsorption in kidneys
Epinephrine, Norepinephrine	Adrenal medulla	Increases blood glucose level and heart rate
Glucagon	Pancreas	Stimulates conversion of glycogen to glucose in the liver; increases blood glucose
Insulin		Lowers blood glucose; increases glycogen stores
Somatostatin		Supresses secretion of glucagon and insulin
Testosterone	Testes	Maintains male secondary sex characteristics
Estrogen	Ovary/Placenta	Maintains female secondary sex characteristics
Progesterone		Promotes growth/maintenance of endometrium
Melatonin	Pineal	Regulates sleep–wake cycles
Atrial natriuretic peptide	Heart	Involved in osmoregulation and vasodilation
Thymosin	Thymus	Stimulates T-cell development

Four Stages of Menstrual Cycle:

1. **Follicular:** FSH causes growth of a follicle
2. **Ovulation:** LH causes follicle to release egg
3. **Luteal:** corpus luteum forms
4. **Menstruation:** endometrial lining sheds

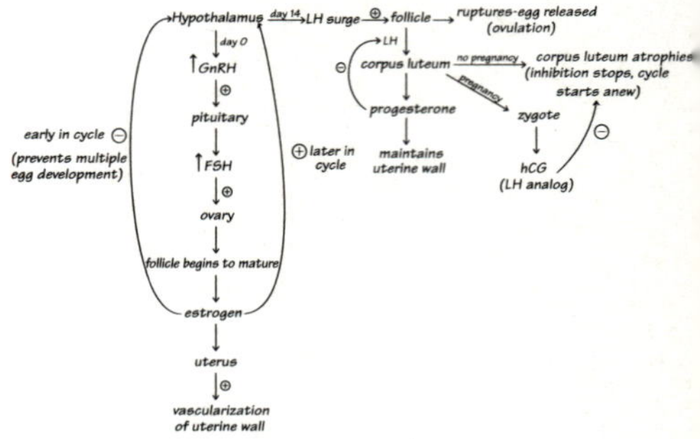

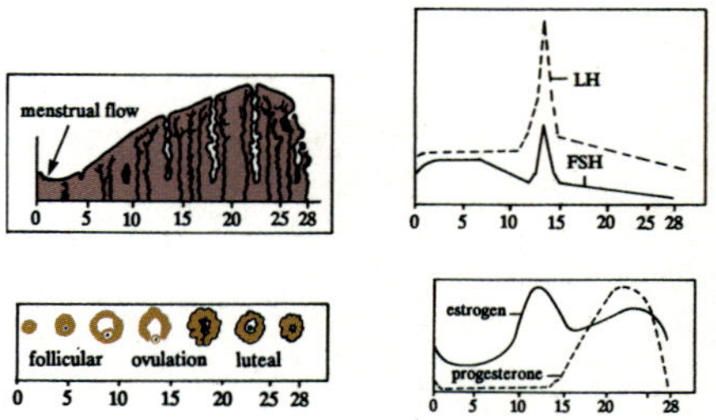

NERVOUS SYSTEM

The functional unit is the neuron:

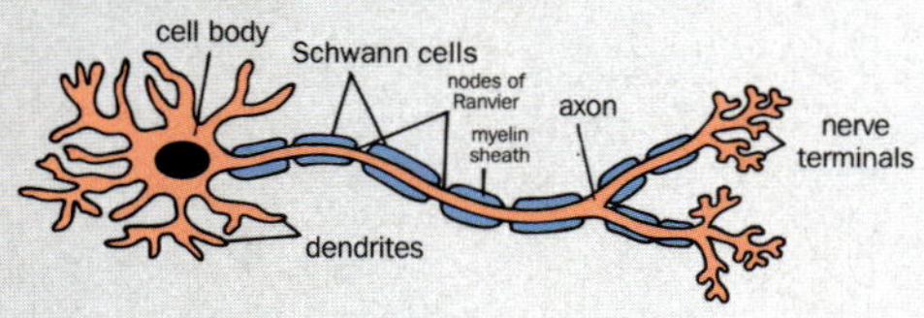

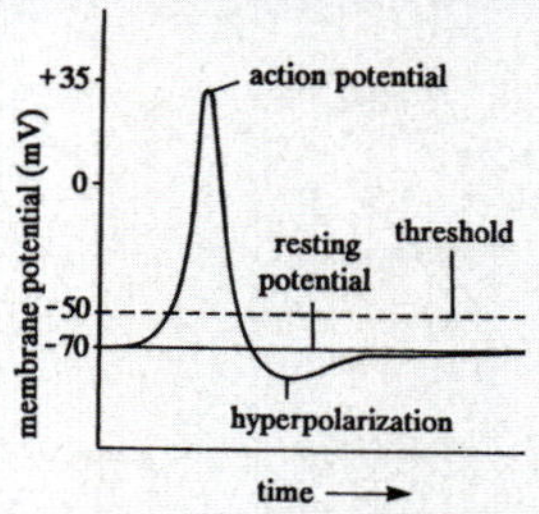

I	Rest	All gates closed
II	Depolarization	Na^+ gates open
III	Repolarization	Na^+ gates inactivate K^+ gates open
IV	Hyperpolarization	All gates closed

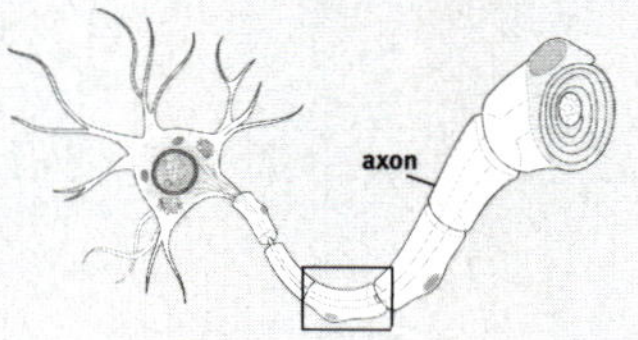

Resting Potential:

- 3 Na^+ pumped out for every 2 K^+ pumped in

Action Potential:

- Stimulus acts on the neuron, depolarizing the membrane of the cell body

Impulse Propagation:

- Depolarization (Na^+ rushing into axon) followed by repolarization (K^+ rushing out of axon) along the nerve axon

The Synapse:

- At the synaptic knob, voltage-gated Ca^{2+} channels open, sending Ca^{2+} into the cell.
- Vesicles fuse with presynaptic membrane sending the neurotransmitter across the **synaptic cleft**.
- Neurotransmitter binds to receptors on the postsynaptic membrane, triggering depolarization.

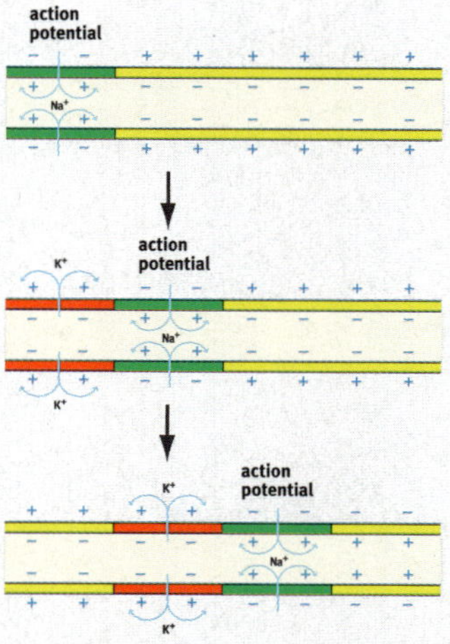

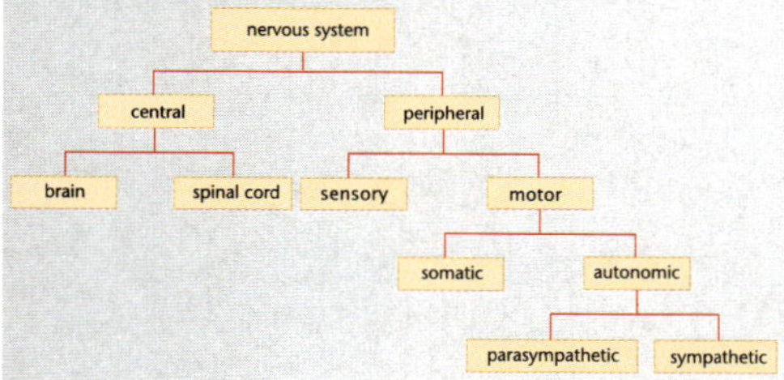

MUSCULOSKELETAL SYSTEM

Sarcomere

- Contractile unit of the fibers in skeletal muscle
- Contains thin actin and thick myosin filaments

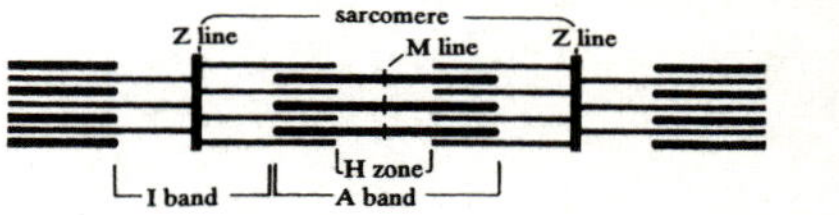

Contraction

Initiation:

- Depolarization of a neuron leads to an action potential.

Sarcomere shortening:

- Sarcoplasmic reticulum releases Ca^{2+}.
- Ca^{2+} binds to troponin on the actin filament.
- Tropomyosin shifts, exposing myosin-binding sites.
- Myosin binds, ATPase activity allows myosin to pull thin filaments towards the center of the H zone, and then ATP causes dissociation.

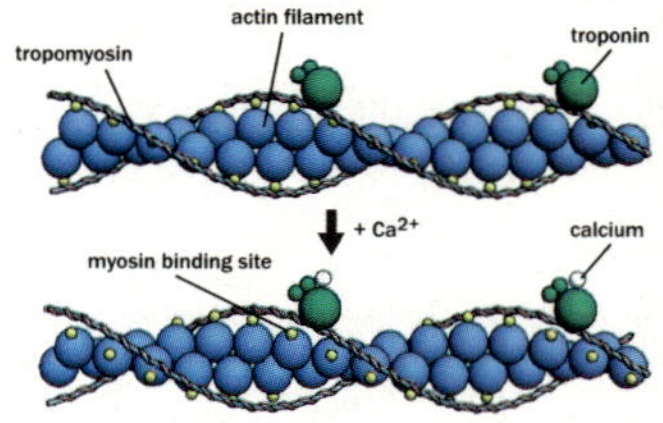

Relaxation:

- Ca^{2+} is pumped back into the sarcoplasmic reticulum.

Bone Formation and Remodeling

- **Osteoblast:** builds bone
- **Osteoclast:** breaks down bone
- **Reformation:** inorganic ions are absorbed from the blood for use in bone
- **Degradation (resorption):** inorganic ions are released into the blood

CIRCULATION

Circulatory Pathway Through Heart

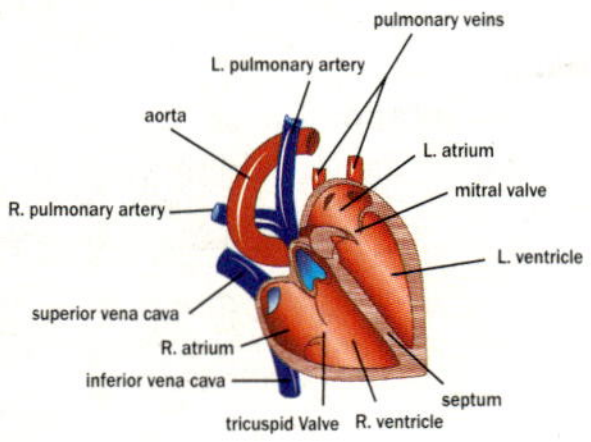

Superior and inferior vena cava → right atrium → right ventricle → pulmonary arteries → lungs→ pulmonary veins → left atrium → left ventricle → aorta → body

Three portal systems: Blood travels through an extra capillary bed before returning to the heart.

- Liver (hepatic), kidney, and brain (hypophyseal)

Fetal Circulation

- **Foramen ovale:** connects right and left atria
- **Ductus arteriosus:** connects pulmonary artery to aorta. Along with foramen ovale, shunts blood away from lungs
- **Ductus venosus:** connects umbilical vein to inferior vena cava, connecting umbilical circulation to central circulation

Blood Components

Plasma: aqueous mixture of nutrients, wastes, hormones, blood proteins, gases, and salts

Erythrocytes (red blood cells): carry oxygen

- Hemoglobin: four subunits carry O_2 and CO_2. Iron controls binding and releasing.
- Oxygen–hemoglobin dissociation:

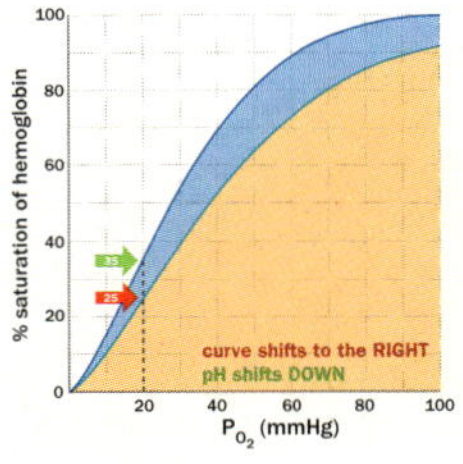

Factors leading to right shift of curve:

- ↑ Temperature
- **Bohr Effect**

  ↓ pH, ↑ P_{CO_2}
- O_2 release to tissues enhanced when H^+ allosterically binds to Hb. ↑ P_{CO_2} leads to ↑ $[H^+]$:

$$CO_2 + H_2O \underset{}{\overset{\text{carbonic anhydrase}}{\rightleftharpoons}} H_2CO_3 \rightleftharpoons H^+ + HCO_3^-$$

Leukocytes (white blood cells): function in immunity

Platelets: clotting

- Platelets release thromboplastin, which (along with cofactors calcium and vitamin K) converts inactive prothrombin to active thrombin.
- Thrombin converts fibrinogen into fibrin, which surrounds blood cells to form the clot.

Blood Typing

Antigens are located on the surface of red blood cells.

Blood type	RBC antigen	Antibodies	Donates to:	Receives From:
A	A	anti-B	A, AB	A, O
B	B	anti-A	B, AB	B, O
AB	A, B	None	AB only	All
O	None	anti-A, B	All	O only

Blood cells with Rh factor are Rh^+; these individuals produce no anti-Rh antibody. Rh^- blood cells lack the antigen; these individuals produce an antibody if exposed.

RESPIRATION

Gas Exchange

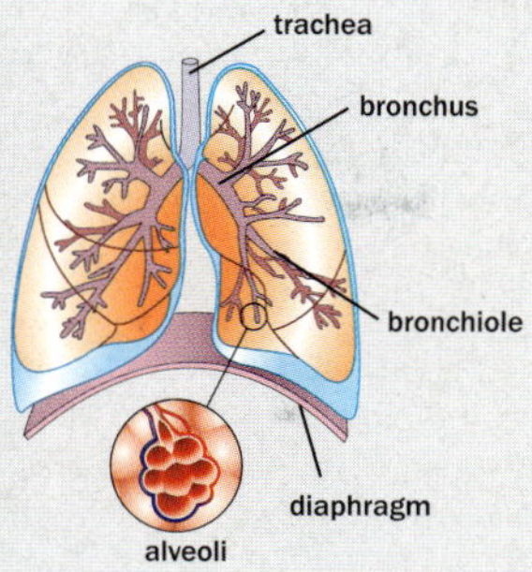

- Exchange occurs across the thin walls of **alveoli.**
- Deoxygenated blood enters the pulmonary capillaries that surround the alveoli.
- O_2 from the inhaled air diffuses down its gradient into the capillaries, where it binds with hemoglobin and returns to the heart.
- CO_2 from the tissues diffuses from the capillaries to the alveoli, and is exhaled.

Fetal Respiration

- Fetal hemoglobin has a higher affinity for oxygen than adult hemoglobin.
- Gas and nutrient exchanges occur across the placenta.

DIGESTION

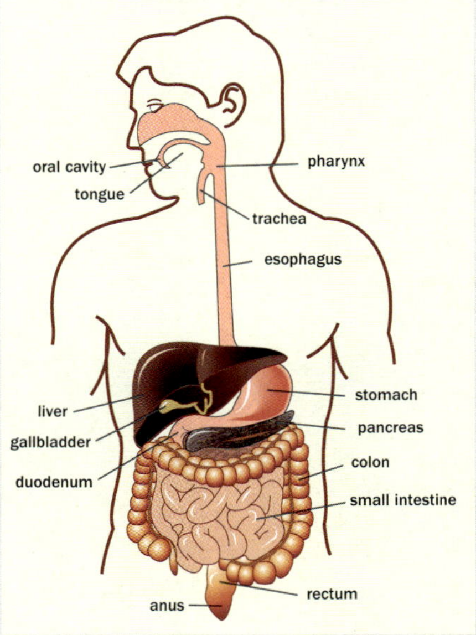

IMMUNE SYSTEM

- The body distinguishes between "self" and "nonself" (antigens).

Humoral Immunity (Specific Defense)

B-lymphocytes → **memory cells** remember antigen, speed up secondary response; → **plasma cells** make and release antibodies (**IgG, IgA, IgM, IgD, IgE**), which induce antigen phagocytosis

- **Active imumunity:** antibodies are produced during an immune response
- **Passive immunity:** antibodies produced by one organism are transferred to another organism

Cell-Mediated Immunity (Specific Defense)

T-lymphocytes →

- **cytotoxic T-cells** destroy cells directly
- **helper T-cells** activate B- and T-cells and macrophages by secreting lymphokines
- **suppressor T-cells** regulate B- and T-cells to decrease anti-antigen activity
- **memory cells**

Nonspecific Immune Response

Includes skin, passages lined with cilia, macrophages, inflammatory response, and interferons (proteins that help prevent the spread of a virus)

Lymphatic System

- Lymph vessels meet at the thoracic duct in the upper chest and neck, draining into the left subclavian vein of the cardiovascular system.
- Vessels carry **lymph** (excess interstitial fluid), and **lacteals** collect fats by absorbing chylomicrons in the small intestine.
- **Lymph nodes** are swellings along the vessels with phagocytic cells (macrophages); they remove foreign particles from lymph.

Lipid Digestion

- When chyme is present, the duodenum secretes the hormone cholecystokinin (CCK) into the blood.
- CCK stimulates the secretion of pancreatic enzymes and bile, and promotes satiety.
- Bile is made in the liver and emulsifies fat in the small intestine; it's not an enzyme.
- Lipase is an enzyme made in the pancreas that hydrolyzes lipids in the small intestine.

Carbohydrate Digestion

Enzyme	Production Site	Function Site	Hydrolysis Reaction
Salivary amylase (ptyalin)	Salivary glands	Mouth	Starch → maltose
Pancreatic amylase	Pancreas	Small intestine	Starch → maltose
Maltase	Intestinal glands	Small intestine	Maltose → 2 glucoses
Sucrase	Intestinal glands	Small intestine	Sucrose → glucose, fructose
Lactase	Intestinal glands	Small intestine	Lactose → glucose, galactose

Protein Digestion

Enzyme	Production Site	Function Site	Function
Pepsin	Gastric glands (chief cells)	Stomach	Hydrolyzes specific peptide bonds
Trypsin	Pancreas	Small Intestine	Hydrolyzes specific peptide bonds Converts chymotrypsinogen to chymotrypsin
Chymotrypsin	Pancreas	Small Intestine	Hydrolyzes specific peptide bonds
Carboxypeptidases A and B	Pancreas	Small Intestine	Hydrolyzes terminal peptide bond at C-terminus
Aminopeptidase	Intestinal glands	Small Intestine	Hydrolyzes terminal peptide bond at N-terminus
Dipeptidases	Intestinal glands	Small Intestine	Hydrolyzes part of amino acids
Enteropeptidase	Intestinal glands	Small Intestine	Converts trypsinogen and procarboxypeptidases to active form

CLASSICAL GENETICS

Law of segregation: Homologous alleles (chromosomes) separate so that each gamete has one copy of each gene.

- If both parents are Rr, the alleles separate to give a genotypic ratio of 1:2:1 and a phenotypic ratio of 3:1.

Law of independent assortment: Alleles of unlinked genes assort independently in meiosis.

- For two traits: AaBb parents will produce AB, Ab, aB, and ab gametes.
- The phenotypic ratio for this cross is 9:3:3:1.

Statistical Calculations

- The probability of producing a genotype that requires multiple events to occur equals the *product* of the probability of each event.
- The probability of producing a genotype that can be the result of multiple different events equals the *sum* of each probability minus the probability of multiple events occurring.

Genetic Mapping

- Crossing over during meiosis I can unlink genes (prophase I).
- Genes are most likely unlinked when far apart.
- One map unit is 1% recombinant frequency (1 centimorgan).

Given recombination frequencies

X and Y: 8%

X and Z: 12%

Y and Z: 4%

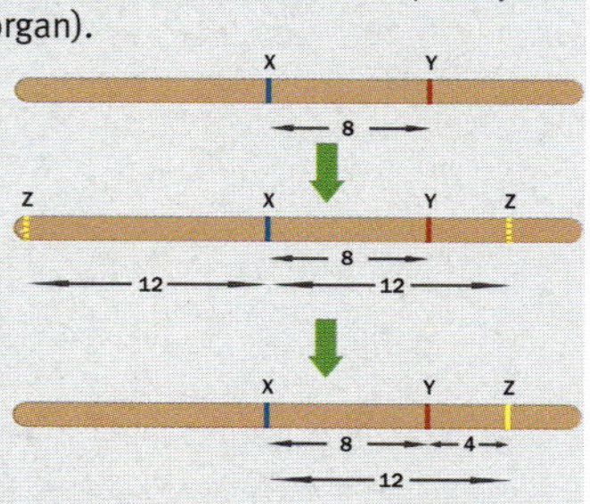

Patterns of Inheritance

- Autosomal recessive: may skip generations
- Autosomal dominant: appears in every generation
- X-linked (sex-linked): no male-to-male transmission, and more males are affected

EVOLUTION

- When frequencies are stable, the population is in **Hardy–Weinberg equilibrium:** no mutations, large population, random mating, no migration, and equal reproductive success

$$p + q = 1;\ p^2 + 2pq + q^2 = 1$$

p = frequency of dominant allele

q = frequency of recessive allele

p^2 = frequency of dominant homozygotes

$2pq$ = frequency of heterozygotes

q^2 = frequency of recessive homozygotes

MOLECULAR GENETICS

Nucleic Acids

- Basic unit: nucleotide (sugar, nitrogenous base, phosphate)
- DNA's sugar: deoxyribose; RNA's sugar: ribose
- 2 types of bases: double-ringed purines (adenine, guanine) and single-ringed pyrimidines (cytosine, uracil, thymine)
- DNA double helix: antiparallel strands joined by base pairs (A=T, G≡C)
- RNA is usually single-stranded: A pairs with U, not T

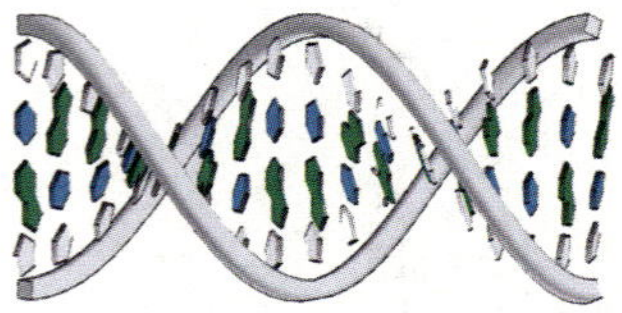

Transcriptional Regulation (Prokaryotes)

Regulated by the **operon:**

- **Structural genes:** have DNA that codes for protein
- **Operator gene:** repressor binding site
- **Promoter gene:** RNA polymerase's 1st binding site
- **Inducible systems** need an inducer for transcription to occur. **Repressible systems** need a corepressor to inhibit transcription.

Mutations

- **Point:** One nucleotide is substituted by another; they are silent if the sequence of amino acids doesn't change.
- **Frameshift:** Insertions or deletions shift reading frame. Protein doesn't form, or is nonfunctional.

Viruses

- Acellular structures of double- or single-stranded DNA or RNA in a protein coat
- **Lytic cycle:** virus kills the host cell
- **Lysogenic cycle:** virus enters host genome

GENETICS OF PROKARYOTIC CELLS

Many bacteria contain **plasmids**, or extragenomic material. Plasmids that can be integrated into the genome are known as **episomes**.

- **Transformation** occurs when a bacterium acquires a piece of genetic material from the environment and integrates that piece of genetic material into the host cell genome. This is a common method by which antibiotic resistance can be acquired.
- **Conjugation** is the bacterial form of mating (sexual reproduction). It involves two cells forming a cytoplasmic bridge between them that allows for the transfer of genetic material. The transfer is one-way, from the donor male (+) to the recipient female (–). The bridge is made from appendages called **sex pili** that are found on the donor male. To form the pilus, bacteria must contain plasmids known as **sex factors**.
- **Transduction** occurs when a bacteriophage acquires genetic information from a host cell. Sometimes, when the new virions are assembled in a host cell, some of the genetic material from the host cell is packaged along with the viral genetic material. Then, the bacteriophage infects another bacterium, resulting in transfer of bacterial genetic material.

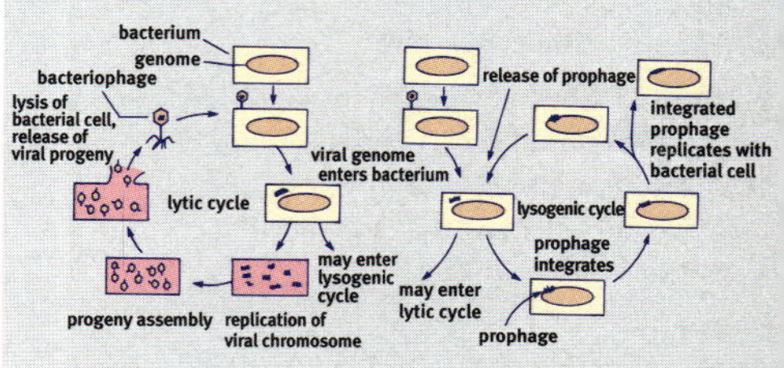

DATA ANALYSIS

A researcher performed the following experiments in order to investigate the metabolism of two different strains of bacteria, Strain 1 and Strain 2.

Experiment 1

Strains 1 and 2 were incubated in separate broth cultures for 24 hours at 37°C. A sample of each culture was streaked onto three different plates—A, B, and C—each containing a different starch–agar medium; the plates were then incubated for another 48 hours at 37°C. The plates were then examined for surface colony growth and stained with iodine solution to determine the extent of starch digestion.

Table 1

	Surface Colony Growth			Starch Digestion		
	A	B	C	A	B	C
Strain 1	+	+	+	–	–	–
Strain 2	+	+	–	+	+	–

key: + = growth/digestion; – = no growth/digestion

Experiment 2

The two strains were incubated in the same manner as in Experiment 1. Two 100 mL portions of agar were poured into two beakers, which were maintained at 43°C. Next, 0.2 mL of broth culture from Strain 1 was pipetted into the first beaker, and 0.2 mL of broth culture from Strain 2 was pipetted into the second beaker. The agar was swirled around to distribute the bacteria evenly through the media, and then poured onto plates. These plates were incubated for 48 hours at 37°C and then examined for colony growth both on the agar surface and lower down within the oxygen-poor agar layer.

Table 2

	Surface Colony Growth	Deep-Agar Colony Growth
Strain 1	+	–
Strain 2	+	+

key: + = growth; – = no growth

Once incubated, bacteria will grow if nutrients they can metabolize are available. Keep this in mind as you interpret the procedure and results.

Experiment 1 and Table 1: What are the important aspects? **Two strains** (1 and 2) undergo **identical incubation** on **3 plates with different starch agars.** Look at Table 1, one strain at a time. The researcher observes growth and starch digestion. Strain 1 grows on all plates, but doesn't digest the starch: it must be using another nutrient to grow. We don't know that Strain 1 *can't* digest starch—we just know that it's not digesting it during these 48 hours. Strain 2 uses starch to grow on plates A and B, but doesn't digest starch or grow on plate C. Again, we don't know that Strain 2 *can't* digest the starch in medium C—we just know it's not doing so during these 48 hours.

Experiment 2 and Table 2: Note the significant differences between the two experiments. This time, the strains were **separately** distributed **within the agar** instead of jointly streaked on top of multiple agars. The researcher observes growth on top and within, the assumption being that the top is oxygen-rich and within is oxygen-poor. What does it mean that Strain 1 only grows in an oxygen-rich environment? It is an obligate aerobe that requires oxygen for metabolism. What does it mean that Strain 2 can grow in oxygen-rich *and* oxygen-poor environments? It is a facultative or aerotolerant anaerobe.

ATOMIC STRUCTURE

Atomic weight: The weighted average of the masses of the naturally occurring isotopes of an element, in amu per atom

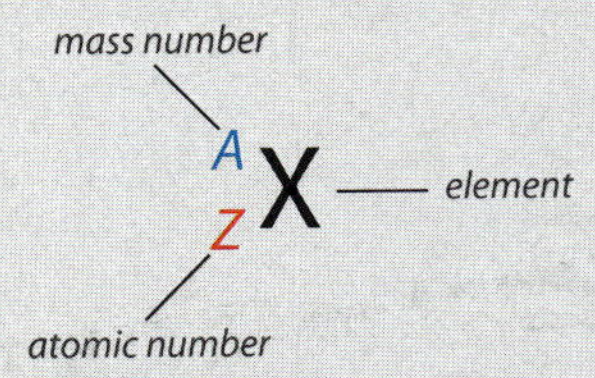

A **mole** is a unit used to count particles and is represented by **Avogadro's number**, 6.022×10^{23} particles.

$$\text{Moles} = \frac{\text{mass of a sample}}{\text{molar mass}}$$

Isotopes: For a given element, multiple species of atoms with the same number of protons (same atomic number) but different numbers of neutrons (different mass numbers)

Planck's quantum theory: Energy emitted as electromagnetic radiation from matter exists in discrete bundles called quanta.

Bohr's Model of the Hydrogen Atom

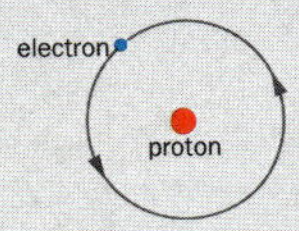

Energy of electron = $E = \frac{-R_H}{n^2}$

Electromagnetic energy of photons = $E = \frac{hc}{\lambda}$

The group of hydrogen emission lines corresponding to transitions from upper levels $n > 2$ to $n = 2$ is known as the **Balmer series**, while the group corresponding to transitions between upper levels $n > 1$ to $n = 1$ is known as the **Lyman series.**

Absorption spectrum: Characteristic energy bands where electrons absorb energy

Quantum Mechanical Model of Atoms

Heisenberg uncertainty principle: It is impossible to determine with perfect accuracy the momentum and the position of an electron simultaneously.

Quantum Numbers:

#	Character	Symbol	Value
1st	Shell	n	n
2nd	Subshell	l	From zero to $n - 1$
3rd	Orbital	m_l	Between l and $-l$
4th	Spin	m_s	$+\frac{1}{2}$ or $-\frac{1}{2}$

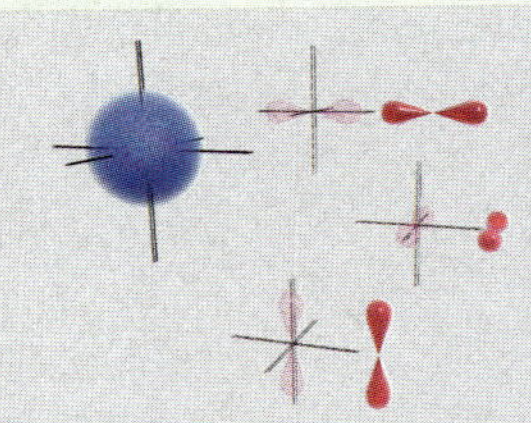

Principal quantum number (n): The larger the integer value of n, the higher the energy level and radius of the electron's orbit. The maximum number of electrons in energy level n is $2n^2$.

Azimuthal quantum number (l): Refers to subshells. The four subshells corresponding to $l = 0, 1, 2,$ and 3 are known as s, p, d, and f, respectively. The maximum number of electrons that can exist within a subshell is given by the equation $4l + 2$.

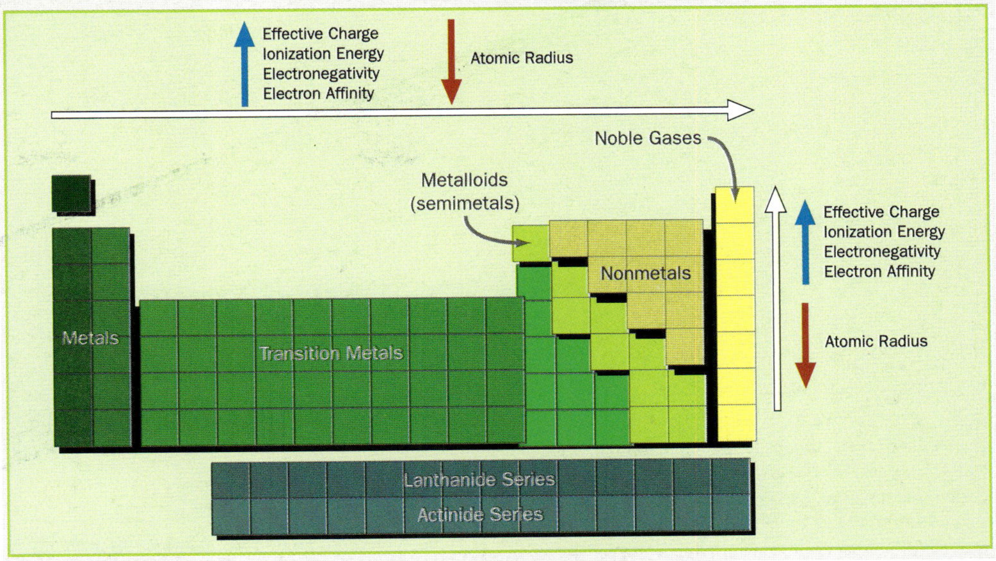

BONDING & CHEMICAL INTERACTIONS

Octet Rule:

- An atom will bond until it has a full outermost shell.
- An atom wants to have a configuration similar to that of Group VIII (noble gases).

Exceptions: Some elements are stable with fewer than 8 electrons: H (2), He (2), Li (2), Be (4), B (6). Atoms found in or beyond the third period can have more than eight valence electrons because some of the valence electrons may occupy d-orbitals. These atoms can have more than four bonds in Lewis structures.
For instance, the sulfate ion can be drawn in at least six resonance forms, many of which have two double bonds attached to a different combination of oxygen atoms.

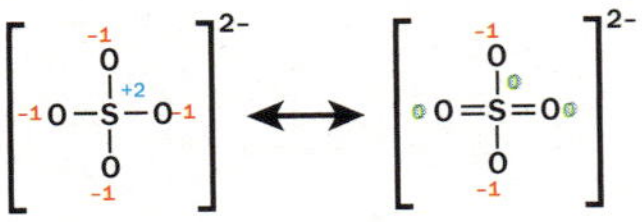

Magnetic quantum number (m_l): This specifies the particular orbital within a subshell where an electron is highly likely to be found at a given point in time.

Spin quantum number (m_s): The spin of a particle is its intrinsic angular momentum and is a characteristic of the particle, like its charge.

Electron Configuration

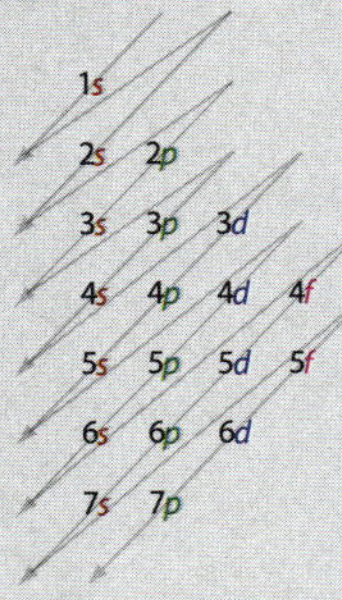

Hund's rule: Within a given subshell, orbitals are filled such that there are a maximum number of half-filled orbitals with parallel spins.

Valence electrons: Electrons of an atom that are in its outer energy shell and that are available for bonding.

Covalent Bond Notation

Lewis structure: The chemical symbol of an element surrounded by dots, each representing one of the s or p valence electrons of the atom.

Steps for drawing Lewis structures:

1. Write the skeletal structure of the compound.
   H–C–N
2. Count all the valence electrons of the atoms.
3. Draw single bonds between the central atom and the atoms surrounding it.
   H : C : N
4. Complete the octets of all atoms bonded to the central atom, using the remaining valence electrons still to be assigned.
   H : C : N̈ :
5. Place any extra electrons on the central atom.
   H − C ≡ N̈

Formal Charges

Formal charge is the charge an atom would have if all the electrons in bonds were shared equally.

Geometry and polarity of covalent molecules

Polar covalent bond: Bonding electron pair is not shared equally, but pulled toward more electronegative atom

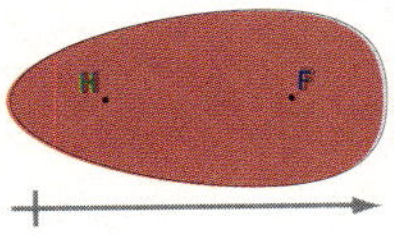

Polarity of molecules: Depends on the polarity of the constituent bonds and on the shape of the molecule. A molecule with nonpolar bonds is always nonpolar; a molecule with polar bonds may be polar or nonpolar depending on the orientation of the bond dipoles.

The overall shape of the molecule determines whether the molecule is in fact polar or not. For instance, the four bond dipoles for the CCl_4 molecule point to the vertices of the tetrahedron and cancel each other.

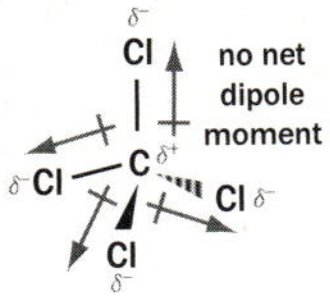

Regions of Electron Density	Example	Geometric Arrangement of Electron Pairs around the Central Atom	Shape	Angle between Electron Pairs
2	$BeCl_2$	X—A—X	linear	180°
3	BH_3		trigonal planar	120°
4	CH_4	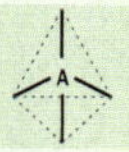	tetrahedral	109.5°
5	PCl_5	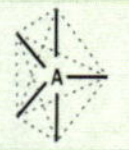	trigonal bipyramidal	90°, 120°, 180°
6	SF_6	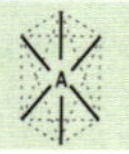	octahedral	90°, 180°

Complex Ion (Coordination Compound)

A Lewis acid–base adduct with a cation bonded to at least one electron pair donor (including water). Donor molecules are called **ligands** and use **coordinate covalent bonds**. The central cation can be bonded to the same ligand multiple times in a process called **chelation**.

Intermolecular Forces

1. **Hydrogen bonding:** The partial positive charge of the hydrogen atom interacts with the partial negative charge located on the electronegative atoms (F, O, N) of nearby molecules.

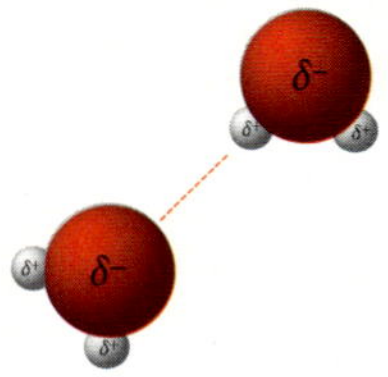

2. **Dipole–dipole interactions:** Polar molecules orient themselves such that the positive region of one molecule is close to the negative region of another molecule.

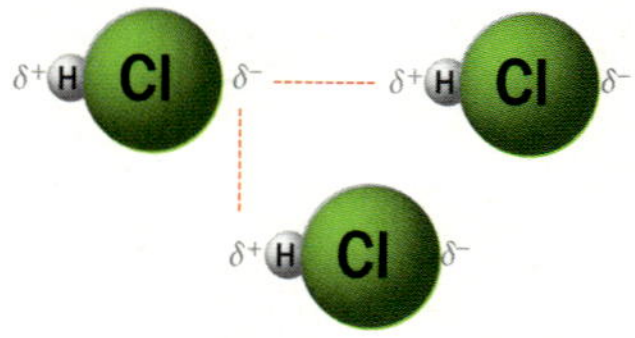

3. **Dispersion forces:** The bonding electrons in covalent bonds may appear to be equally shared between two atoms, but at any particular point in time they will be located randomly throughout the orbital. This permits unequal sharing of electrons, causing transient polarization and counterpolarization of the electron clouds of neighboring molecules, inducing the formation of more dipoles.

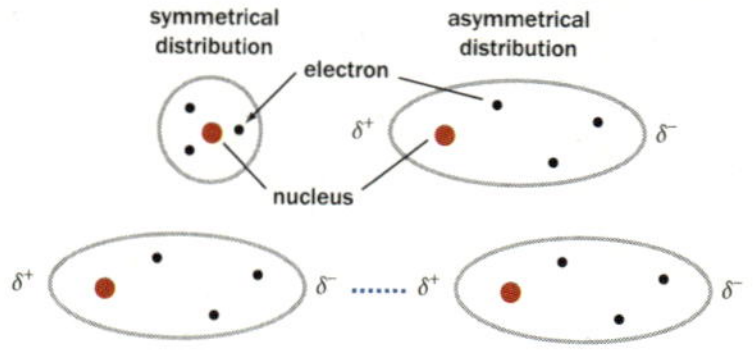

KINETICS & EQUILIBRIUM

Experimental determination of rate law: The values of k, x, and y in the rate law equation (rate = $k[A]^x[B]^y$) must be determined experimentally for a given reaction at a given temperature. The rate is usually measured as a function of the initial concentrations of the reactants, A and B.

Efficiency of Reactions

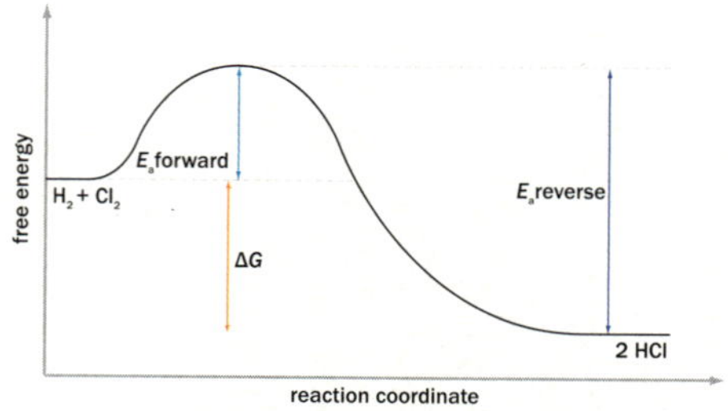

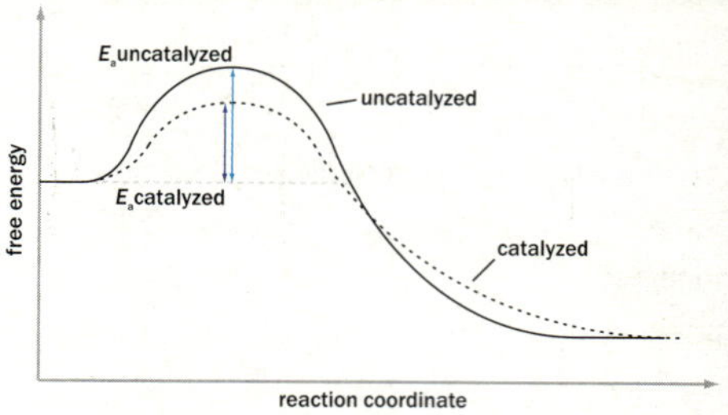

Law of Mass Action

$$aA + bB \rightleftharpoons cC + dD$$

$$K_c = \frac{[C]^c[D]^d}{[A]^a[B]^b}$$

K_c is the equilibrium constant (c stands for concentration).

Properties of the Equilibrium Constant

Pure solids and liquids don't appear in expressions.

K_{eq} is characteristic of a given system at a given temperature.

If $K_{eq} \gg 1$, an equilibrium mixture of reactants and products will contain very little of the reactants compared to the products.

If $K_{eq} \ll 1$, an equilibrium mixture of reactants and products will contain very little of the products compared to the reactants.

If K_{eq} is close to 1, an equilibrium mixture of products and reactants will contain approximately equal amounts of the two.

Le Châtelier's principle is used to determine the direction in which a reaction at equilibrium will proceed when subjected to a stress, such as a change in concentration, pressure, volume, or temperature. The key is to remember that a system to which these kinds of stresses are applied tends to change so as to relieve the applied stress.

In a nutshell:

A + B ⇌ C + heat	
Will shift to **RIGHT**	Will shift to **LEFT**
1. If more A or B added	1. If more C added
2. If C taken away	2. If A or B taken away
3. If pressure applied or volume reduced (assuming A, B, and C are gases)	3. If pressure reduced or volume increased (assuming A, B, and C are gases)
4. If temperature reduced	4. If temperature increased

COMPOUNDS & STOICHIOMETRY

A **mole** is the amount of a substance that contains the same number of particles that are found in a 12.000 g sample of carbon-12.

The **molecular** or **formula weight** is measured in amu per molecule (or formula unit). The **molar mass** is measured in grams per mole.

Combustion reactions: A fuel, such as a hydrocarbon, is reacted with an oxidant, such as oxygen, to produce an oxide and water.

$$CH_4\,(g) + 2\,O_2\,(g) \rightarrow CO_2\,(g) + 2\,H_2O\,(g)$$

Combination reactions: Two or more reactants form one product.

$$S\,(s) + O_2\,(g) \rightarrow SO_2\,(g)$$

Decomposition reactions: A compound breaks down into two or more substances, usually as a result of heating or electrolysis.

$$2\,HgO\,(s) \rightarrow 2\,Hg\,(l) + O_2\,(g)$$

Single-displacement reactions: An atom (or ion) of one compound is replaced by an atom of another element.

$$Zn\,(s) + CuSO_4\,(aq) \rightarrow Cu\,(s) + ZnSO_4\,(aq)$$

Double-displacement reactions: Also called metathesis reactions; elements from two different compounds displace each other to form two new compounds.

$$CaCl_2\,(aq) + 2\,AgNO_3\,(aq) \rightarrow Ca(NO_3)_2\,(aq) + 2\,AgCl\,(s)$$

Net ionic equations: These types of equations are written showing only the species that actually participate in the reaction. Consider the following equation:

$$Zn\,(s) + Cu^{2+}\,(aq) + SO_4^{2-}\,(aq) \rightarrow Cu\,(s) + Zn^{2+}\,(aq) + SO_4^{2-}\,(aq)$$

The spectator ion (SO_4^{2-}) does not take part in the overall reaction, but simply remains in solution throughout. The net ionic equation would be:

$$Zn\,(s) + Cu^{2+}\,(aq) \rightarrow Cu\,(s) + Zn^{2+}\,(aq)$$

Neutralization reactions: These are specific double-displacement reactions that occur when an acid reacts with a base to produce a solution of a salt (and, usually, water):

$$HCl\,(aq) + NaOH\,(aq) \rightarrow NaCl\,(aq) + H_2O\,(l)$$

Factors affecting reaction rates: reactant concentrations, temperature, medium, catalysts

Catalysts are unique substances that increase reaction rate without being consumed; they do this by lowering the activation energy.

THERMOCHEMISTRY

The law of conservation of energy dictates that energy can be neither created nor destroyed, but that all thermal, chemical, potential, and kinetic energies are interconvertible.

Systems:

Isolated: no exchange of energy/matter with the environment. Bomb calorimetry creates a nearly isolated system.

Closed: can exchange energy but not matter with the environment

Open: can exchange both energy and matter with the environment. Human beings are open systems because they can take in energy and matter (eat), release matter into the environment (respiration, urination, defecation), and release energy into the environment (heat transfer from the skin and mucous membranes).

System processes:

Isothermal: temperature of system remains constant

Adiabatic: no heat exchange occurs

Isobaric: pressure of system remains constant

Isovolumetric (isochoric): volume remains constant

Heat: the transfer of thermal energy from one object to another

Endothermic: reactions that absorb thermal energy

Exothermic: reactions that release thermal energy

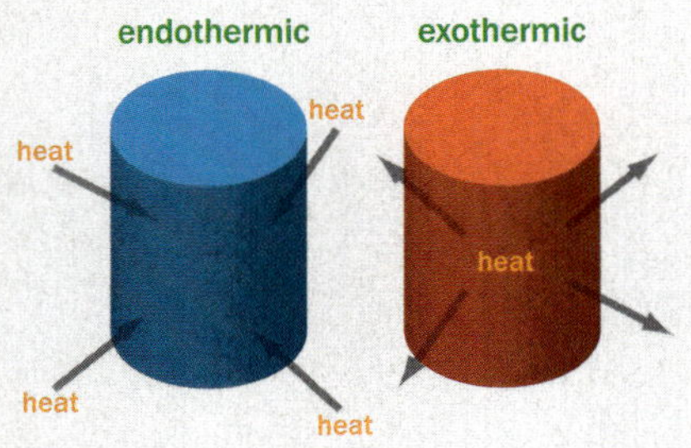

Constant-volume and constant-pressure calorimetry: used to indicate conditions under which the heat flow is measured

$q = mc\Delta T$, where q is the heat absorbed or released in a given process, m is the mass, c is the specific heat, and ΔT is the change in temperature

States and state functions: are described by the macroscopic properties of the system. These properties' magnitudes depend only on the initial and final states of the system, and not on the path of the change. Common state functions include pressure, density, temperature, volume, enthalpy, internal energy, free energy, and entropy.

Enthalpy (H): is used to express heat changes at constant pressure

Standard heat of formation (ΔH°_f): the enthalpy change that would occur if one mole of a compound was formed directly from its elements in their standard states

Standard heat of reaction (ΔH°_{rxn}): the hypothetical enthalpy change that would occur if the reaction were carried out under standard conditions

$$\Delta H^\circ_{rxn} = (\text{sum of } \Delta H^\circ_f \text{ of products}) - (\text{sum of } \Delta H^\circ_f \text{ of reactants})$$

Hess's law: states that enthalpies of reactions are additive

The reverse of any reaction has an enthalpy of the same magnitude as that of the forward reaction, but its sign is opposite.

Bond dissociation energy: an average of the energy required to break a particular type of bond in one mole of gaseous molecules:

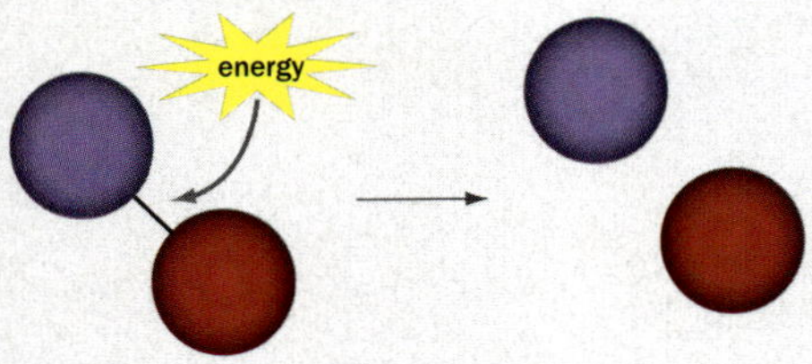

Bond enthalpy: The standard heat of reaction can be calculated using the values of bond dissociation energies of particular bonds (given in a table).

$$\Delta H^\circ_{rxn} = \sum \Delta H_{\text{bonds broken}} - \sum \Delta H_{\text{bonds formed}}$$

THE GAS PHASE

1 atm = 760 mmHg ≡ 760 torr = 101,325 Pa

Do not confuse STP with standard conditions—the two standards involve different temperatures and are used for different purposes. STP (0°C or 273 K, 1 atm) is generally used for gas law calculations; standard conditions (25°C or 298 K, 1 atm, 1 *M* concentrations) is used when measuring standard enthalpy, entropy, Gibbs free energy, and electromotive force.

Boyle's Law

$$PV = k \text{ or } P_1V_1 = P_2V_2$$

Charles's Law

$$\frac{V}{T} = k \text{ or } \frac{V_1}{T_1} = \frac{V_2}{T_2}$$

Gay-Lussac's Law

$$\frac{P}{T} = k \text{ or } \frac{P_1}{T_1} = \frac{P_2}{T_2}$$

Avogadro's Principle

$$\frac{n}{V} = k \text{ or } \frac{n_1}{V_1} = \frac{n_2}{V_2}$$

Combined Gas Law

Integrates Boyle's Law, Charles's Law, and Gay-Lussac's Law

$$\frac{P_1V_1}{T_1} = \frac{P_2V_2}{T_2}$$

Ideal Gas Law

$$PV = nRT$$

Real Gases

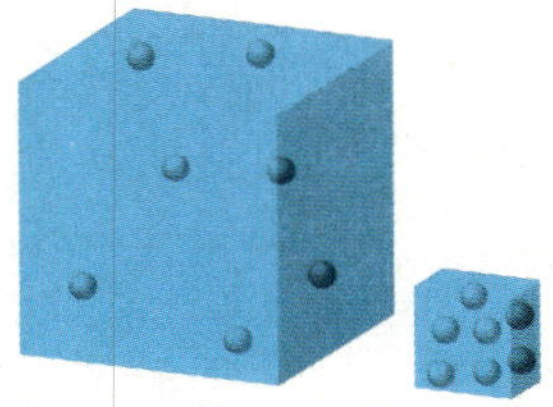

Decreasing the volume of a sample of gas makes it behave less ideally because the individual gas particles are in closer proximity in a smaller volume. (They are more likely to engage in intermolecular interactions.)

Entropy (S): the measure of the distribution of energy ("randomness") throughout a system

$$\Delta S_{universe} = \Delta S_{system} + \Delta S_{surroundings}$$

Gibbs free energy (G): combines the two factors that affect the spontaneity of a reaction—changes in enthalpy, ΔH, and changes in entropy, ΔS

$$\Delta G = \Delta H - T\Delta S$$

If ΔG is negative, the reaction is spontaneous.

If ΔG is positive, the reaction is nonspontaneous.

If ΔG is zero, the system is in a state of equilibrium; thus, $\Delta H = T\Delta S$.

ΔH	ΔS	Outcome
–	+	Spontaneous at all temps.
+	–	Nonspontaneous at all temps.
+	+	Spontaneous only at high temps.
–	–	Spontaneous only at low temps.

Reaction quotient (Q): Once a reaction commences, the standard state conditions no longer hold. For the reaction:

$$a\text{A} + b\text{B} \rightleftharpoons c\text{C} + d\text{D}$$

$$Q = \frac{[\text{C}]^c[\text{D}]^d}{[\text{A}]^a[\text{B}]^b}$$

Deviations due to pressure: As the pressure of a gas increases, the particles are pushed closer and closer together. At moderately high pressure, a gas's volume is less than would be predicted by the ideal gas law due to intermolecular attraction.

Deviations due to temperature: As the temperature of a gas decreases, the average velocity of the gas molecules decreases and the attractive intermolecular forces become increasingly significant. As the temperature of a gas is reduced, intermolecular attraction (a) causes the gas to have a smaller volume than would be predicted. At extremely low temperatures, the volume of the gas particles themselves (b) causes the gas to have a larger volume than would be predicted.

Van der Waals equation of state: accounts for the deviations from ideality that occur when a gas does not closely follow the ideal gas law

$$\left(P + \frac{n^2a}{V^2}\right)(V - nb) = nRT$$

1 mole of gas at STP = 22.4 L

Dalton's law of partial pressures: states that the total pressure of a gaseous mixture is equal to the sum of the partial pressures of the individual components

$$P_T = P_A + P_B + P_C + \ldots$$

$$P_A = P_T X_A$$

$$\text{where } X_A = \frac{n_A}{n_T}\ \frac{(\text{moles of A})}{(\text{total moles})}$$

Kinetic molecular theory of gases: an explanation of gaseous molecular behavior based on the motion of individual molecules

Average molecular speeds

$$K = \frac{1}{2}mv^2 = \frac{3}{2}k_BT$$

Root-mean-square speed

$$u_{rms} = \sqrt{\left(\frac{3RT}{M}\right)}$$

PHASES & PHASE CHANGES

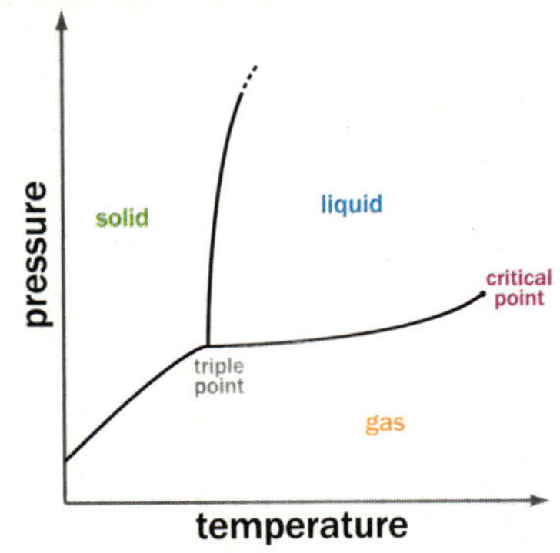

Colligative properties: These are physical properties derived solely from the number of particles present, not the nature of those particles. These properties are usually associated with dilute solutions. Molality (m) is often used, in addition to the van 't Hoff factor (i) for ionic compounds.

Freezing point depression

$$\Delta T_f = iK_f m$$

Boiling point elevation

$$\Delta T_b = iK_b m$$

Osmotic pressure

$$\Pi = MRT$$

Vapor pressure lowering (Raoult's law)

$$P_A = X_A P_A^\circ;\ P_B = X_B P_B^\circ$$

Solutions that obey Raoult's Law are called ideal solutions.

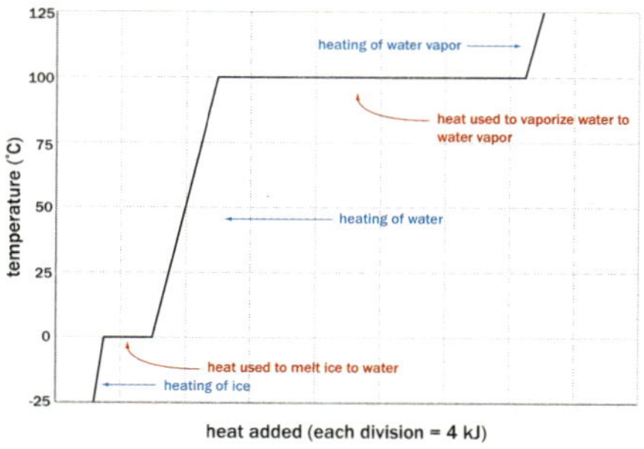

Graham's law of diffusion and effusion

Diffusion: occurs when gas molecules distribute through a volume by random motion

Effusion: the flow of gas particles under pressure from one compartment to another through a small opening:

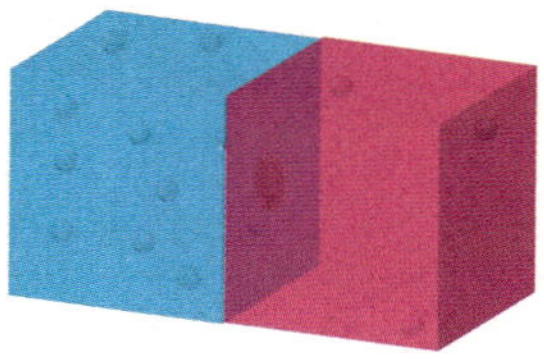

Both diffusion and effusion have the same formula:

$$\frac{r_1}{r_2} = \sqrt{\left(\frac{m_2}{m_1}\right)}$$

SOLUTIONS

1. All salts containing alkali metal (Group 1) or ammonium (NH_4^+) cations are water-soluble.
2. All salts containing the nitrate (NO_3^-) or acetate (CH_3COO^-) anions are water-soluble.
3. All chlorides, bromides, and iodides are water-soluble, with the exception of Ag^+, Pb^{2+}, and Hg^{2+}.
4. All salts of the sulfate ion (SO_4^{2-}) are water-soluble, with the exception of Ca^{2+}, Sr^{2+}, Ba^{2+}, and Pb^{2+}.
5. All metal oxides are insoluble, with the exception of the alkali metals and CaO, SrO, BaO, all of which hydrolyze to form solutions of the corresponding metal hydroxides.
6. All hydroxides are insoluble, with the exception of the alkali metals and Ca^{2+}, Sr^{2+}, and Ba^{2+}.
7. All carbonates (CO_3^{2-}), phosphates (PO_4^{3-}), sulfides (S^{2-}), and sulfites (SO_3^{2-}) are insoluble, with the exception of the alkali metals and ammonium.

Units of Concentration

Percent composition by mass:

$$\frac{\text{Mass of solute}}{\text{Mass of solution}} \times 100\%$$

Mole fraction: $\frac{\text{\# of mol of compound}}{\text{total \# of moles in system}}$

Molarity: $\frac{\text{\# of mol of solute}}{\text{liter of solution}}$

Molality: $\frac{\text{\# of mol of solute}}{\text{kg of solvent}}$

Normality: $\frac{\text{\# of gram equivalent weights of solute}}{\text{liter of solution}}$

ACIDS AND BASES

Arrhenius definition: An acid is a species that produces excess H^+ (protons) in an aqueous solution, and a base is a species that produces excess OH^- (hydroxide ions).

Brønsted–Lowry definition: An acid is a species that donates protons, while a base is a species that accepts protons.

Lewis definition: An acid is an electron pair acceptor, and a base is an electron pair donor.

Properties of Acids and Bases

$$pH = -\log[H^+] = \log\left(\frac{1}{[H^+]}\right)$$

$$pOH = -\log[OH^-] = \log\left(\frac{1}{[OH^-]}\right)$$

$$H_2O\ (l) \rightleftharpoons H^+\ (aq) + OH^-\ (aq)$$

$$K_w = [H^+][OH^-] = 10^{-14}$$

$$pH + pOH = 14$$

Weak Acids and Bases

$$HA\ (aq) + H_2O\ (l) \rightleftharpoons H_3O^+\ (aq) + A^-\ (aq)$$

$$K_a = \frac{[H_3O^+][A^-]}{[HA]}$$

$$K_b = \frac{[B^+][OH^-]}{[BOH]}$$

Salt formation: Acids and bases may react with each other, forming a salt and (often, but not always) water in a neutralization reaction.

$$HA + BOH \rightarrow BA + H_2O$$

Hydrolysis: This is the reverse reaction, where the salt ions react with water to give back the acid and base.

Amphoteric species: is one that can act either as an acid or a base, depending on its chemical environment

Titration and Buffers

Titration is a procedure used to determine the molarity of an acid or base by reacting a known volume of a solution of unknown concentration with a known volume of a solution of known concentration. The half-equivalence point defines $pH = pK_a$

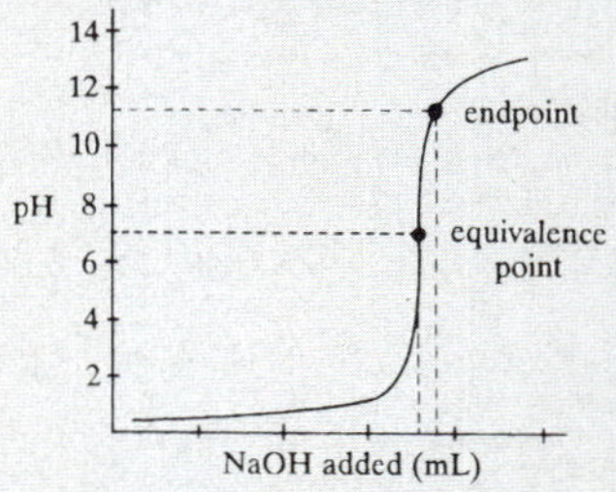

strong acid and strong base

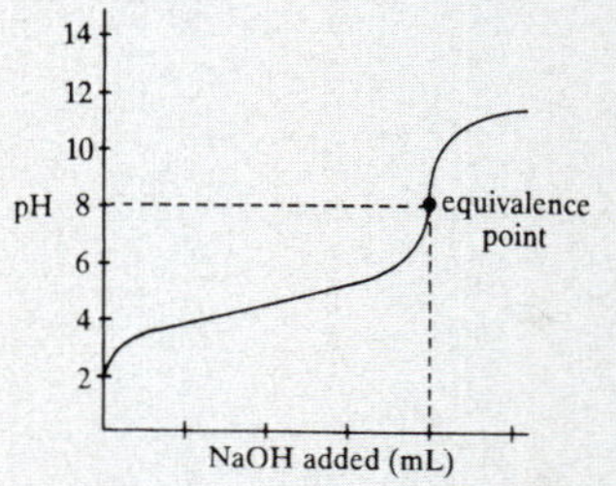

weak acid and strong base

Henderson–Hasselbalch equation: is used to estimate the pH of a solution in the buffer region where the concentrations of the species and its conjugate are present in approximately equal concentrations

$$pH = pK_a + \log\frac{[\text{conjugate base}]}{[\text{weak acid}]}$$

$$pOH = pK_b + \log\frac{[\text{conjugate acid}]}{[\text{weak base}]}$$

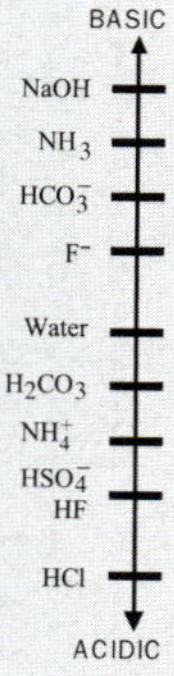

REDOX REACTIONS & ELECTROCHEMISTRY

Oxidation: loss of electrons

Reduction: gain of electrons

Oxidizing agent: causes another atom to undergo oxidation, and is itself reduced

Reducing agent: causes another atom to be reduced, and is itself oxidized

Galvanic Cells

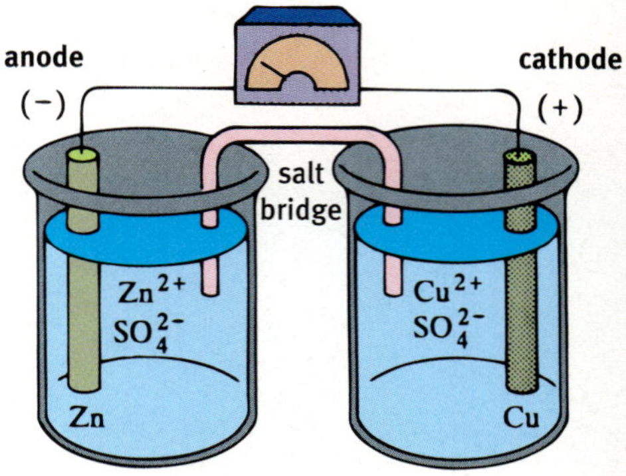

A redox reaction occurring in a galvanic cell has a negative ΔG and is therefore a spontaneous reaction. Galvanic cell reactions supply energy and are used to do work.

This energy can be harnessed by placing the oxidation–reduction half-reactions in separate containers called **half-cells**. The half-cells are then connected by an apparatus that allows for the flow of electrons.

Electrolytic Cells

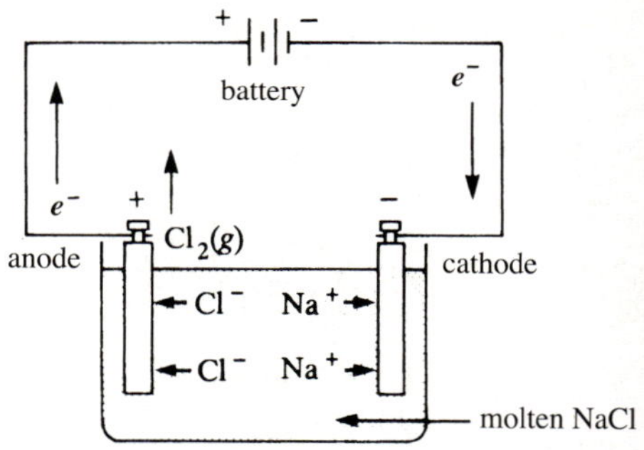

A redox reaction occurring in an electrolytic cell has a positive ΔG and is therefore nonspontaneous. In electrolysis, electrical energy is required to induce a reaction. The oxidation and reduction half-reactions are usually placed in one container.

Reduction potential of each species is defined as the tendency of a species to acquire electrons and be reduced. Standard reduction potential, E°, is measured under standard conditions: 25°C, 1 *M* concentration for each ion in the reaction, a partial pressure of 1 atm for each gas and metals in their pure state.

Standard reduction potentials are used to calculate the standard electromotive force (emf or E°_{cell}) of a reaction, the difference in potential between two half-cells.

$$emf = E^\circ_{red,\ cathode} - E^\circ_{red,\ anode}$$

Gibbs free energy, ΔG, is the thermodynamic criterion for determining the spontaneity of a reaction.

$$\Delta G = -nFE_{cell}$$

NOMENCLATURE

1. Find the longest carbon chain containing the principal functional group (highest-priority groups are generally the most oxidized).
2. Number the carbon chain so that the principal functional group gets lowest possible number.
3. Proceed to number the chain so that the lowest set of numbers is obtained for the substituents.
4. Name the substituents and assign each a number.
5. Complete the name by listing substituents in alphabetical order; place commas between numbers and dashes between numbers and words.

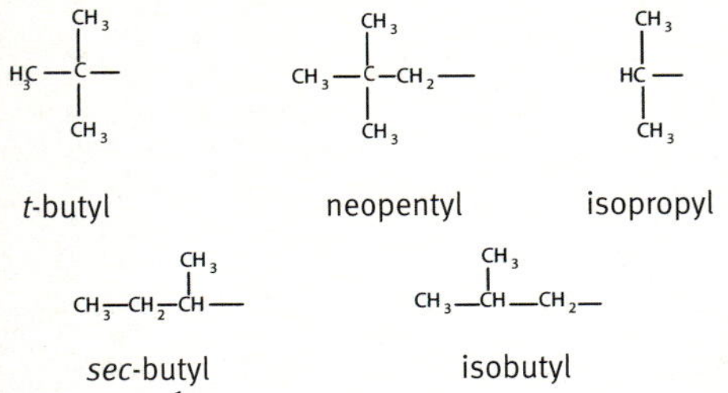

Functional Group	Prefix	Suffix
Carboxylic acid	*carboxy–*	*–oic acid*
Anhydrides	*alkanoyloxy-carbonyl–*	*anhydride*
Esters	*alkoxycarbonyl–*	*–oate*
Amides	*carbomoyl–*	*–amide*
Aldehydes	*oxo–*	*–al*
Ketones	*oxo–* or *keto–*	*–one*
Alcohols	*hydroxy–*	*–ol*

ISOMERS

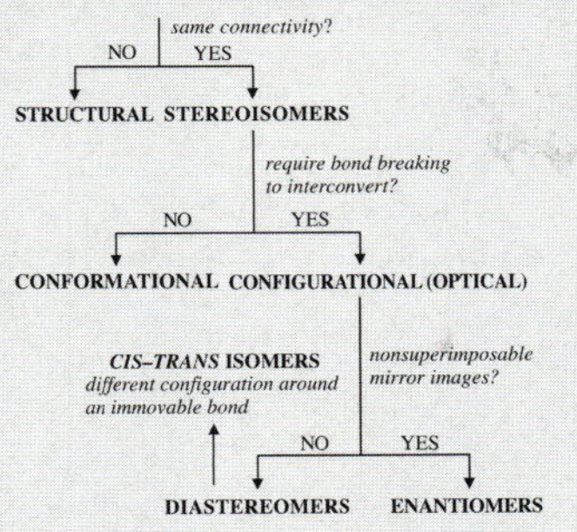

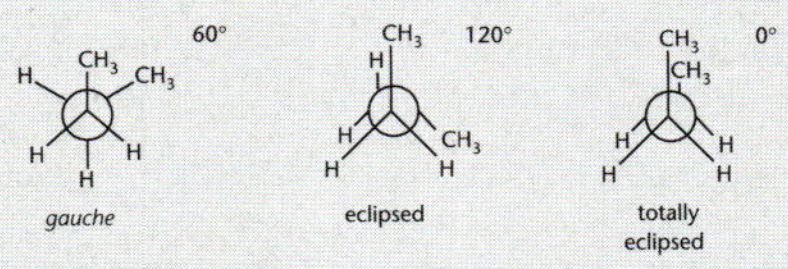

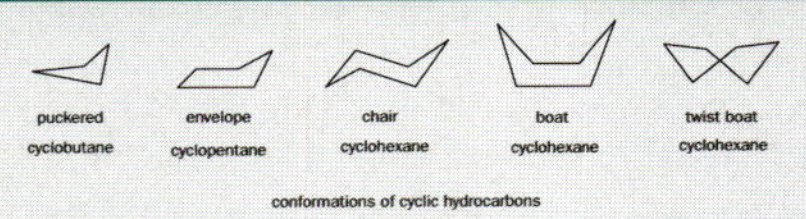

Physical properties are characteristics of processes that don't change the composition of matter, such as melting point, boiling point, solubility, odor, color, and density.

Chemical properties have to do with the reactivity of the molecule with other molecules.

Stereoisomers

Conformational isomers

Differ by rotation around a single (σ) bond

- **Staggered conformations** have groups 60° apart, as seen in a **Newman projection.** ***anti*** = largest groups are 180° apart; ***gauche*** = 60° apart.
- **Eclipsed conformations** have groups directly in front of each other. **Totally eclipsed** = largest groups are directly in front of each other; strain is maximized.

Cyclic Strain

Comes from:

- **Angle strain:** stretch or compress angles from normal size
- **Torsional strain:** from eclipsing conformations
- **Nonbonded strain:** from interactions with substituents on nonadjacent carbons. In cyclohexane, the largest substituent usually takes equatorial position to reduce nonbonded strain

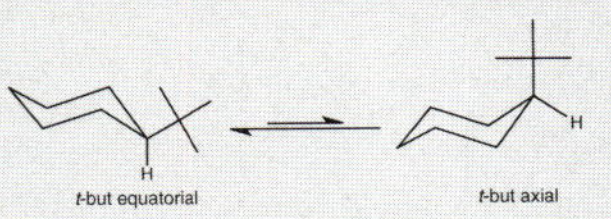

Configurational Isomers

Can only be interchanged by breaking and reforming bonds

- **Enantiomers:** nonsuperimposable mirror images; have opposite stereochemistry at every chiral carbon. Same chemical and physical properties except for rotation of plane-polarized light and reactions in a chiral environment

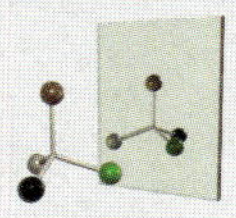

Racemic mixtures and *meso* compounds are optically inactive.

- **Diastereomers:** non-mirror-image stereoisomers. Differ at some, but not all, chiral centers. They have different chemical and physical properties.
- ***Cis–trans:*** subtype of diastereomers in which groups differ in position about an immovable bond (such as a double bond or in a cycloalkane).

Absolute Configuration

An alkene is **(*Z*)** if the highest-priority substituents are on the same side of the double bond, and **(*E*)** if on opposite sides.

A stereocenter's configuration is determined by putting the lowest-priority group in the back and drawing a circle from group 1 to 2 to 3 in descending priority. If this circle is clockwise, the stereocenter is **(*R*)**; if it is counterclockwise, the stereocenter is **(*S*)**.

BONDING

Bond order	single	double	triple
Bond type	σ	σ π	σ 2π
Hybridization	sp^3	sp^2	sp
Angles	109.5°	120°	180°
Example	C–C	C=C	C≡C

ALKANES

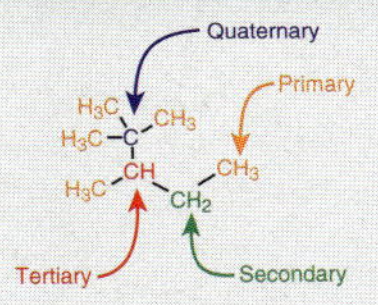

Combustion

$$C_3H_8 + 5\,O_2 \rightarrow 3\,CO_2 + 4\,H_2O + \text{heat}$$

S_N1	S_N2
2 steps	1 step
Favored in polar protic solvents	Favored in polar aprotic solvents
3° › 2° › 1° › methyl	Methyl › 1° › 2° › 3°
rate = *k*[RL]	rate = *k*[Nu][RL]
Racemic products	Optically active and inverted products
Strong nucleophile not required	Favored with strong nucleophile

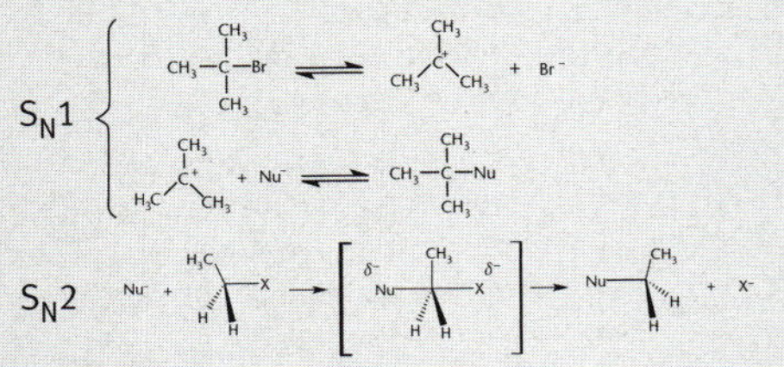

Nucleophiles

Nucleophile = "nucleus-loving"; tend to have lone pairs or π bonds that can form new bonds to electrophiles. Nucleophilicity is increased by increasing electron density.

Nucleophilicity is determined by four major factors:

- Charge: Nucleophilicity increases with increasing electron density (more negative charge).
- Electronegativity: Nucleophilicity decreases as electronegativity increases because these atoms are less likely to share electron density.
- Steric hindrance: Bulkier molecules are less nucleophilic.
- Solvent: Protic solvents can inhibit nucleophilicity by protonating the nucleophile or through hydrogen bonding.

In aprotic solvents, nucleophilicity parallels basicity:

$$F^- > Cl^- > Br^- > I^-$$

In protic solvents, good bases pick up protons and are worse nucleophiles:

$$I^- > Br^- > Cl^- > F^-$$

Electrophiles

Electrophile = "electron-loving"; tend to have a positive charge or positively polarized atom that accepts an electron pair from a nucleophile. Electrophilicity is increased by increasing the positive charge.

Most common electrophiles:

- Carbonyl carbon
- Substrate carbon in an alkane
- Carbocations

Leaving Groups

Leaving groups = molecular fragments that retain the electrons after **heterolysis** (breaking a bond, with both electrons being given to one of the two products). The best leaving groups will be able to stabilize the extra electrons.

Most common leaving groups:

- Weak bases
- Large groups with resonance
- Large groups with electron-withdrawing atoms

DETERMINING ORGANIC MECHANISMS

Step 1: Know Your Nomenclature

If given compound names in a question stem or passage, be able to draw them. If working with reaction diagrams, be able to name the compounds.

Step 2: Identify the Functional Groups

What functional groups are in the molecule? Do these functional groups act as acids or bases? How oxidized is the carbon? Are there functional groups that act as good nucleophiles, electrophiles, or leaving groups? This will help define a category of reactions that can occur with the given functional groups.

Step 3: Identify the Other Reagents

Are the other reagents acidic or basic? Are they specific to a particular reaction? Are they good nucleophiles or a specific solvent? Are they good oxidizing or reducing agents?

Step 4: Identify the Most Reactive Functional Group(s)

More oxidized carbons tend to be more reactive to both nucleophile–electrophile reactions and oxidation–reduction reactions. Note the presence of protecting groups that exist to prevent a particular functional group from reacting.

Step 5: Identify the First Step of the Reaction

- If the reaction involves an acid or a base: protonation or deprotonation
- If the reaction involves a nucleophile: nucleophile attacks electrophile, forming a bond
- If the reaction involves an oxidizing or reducing agent: most oxidized functional group is oxidized or reduced, accordingly

Step 6: Consider Stereoselectivity

If there is more than one product, the major product will generally be determined by differences in strain or stability between the two molecules. Products with **conjugation** (alternating single and multiple bonds) are significantly more stable than those without.

ALCOHOLS

- Higher boiling points than alkanes
- Weakly acidic hydroxyl hydrogen

Synthesis

- Addition of water to double bonds
- S_N1 and S_N2 reactions
- Reduction of carboxylic acids, aldehydes, ketones, and esters
  - Aldehydes and ketones with $NaBH_4$ or $LiAlH_4$
  - Esters and carboxylic acids with $LiAlH_4$

Reactions

Substitution reactions after protonation or leaving group conversion

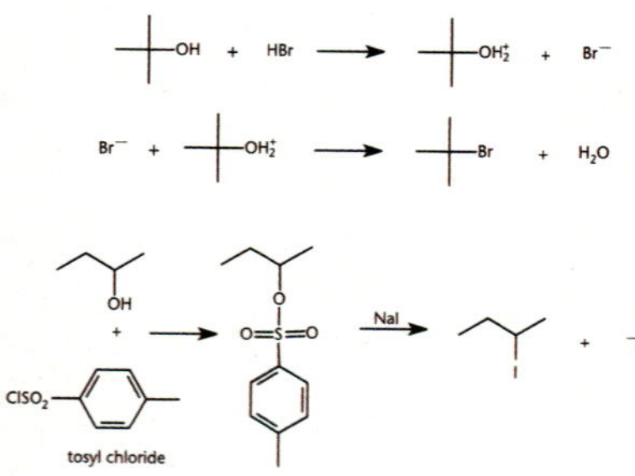

ORGANIC OXIDATION–REDUCTION

- **Level 0** (no bonds to heteroatoms): alkanes
- **Level 1**: alcohols, alkyl halides, amines
- **Level 2**: aldehydes, ketones, imines
- **Level 3**: carboxylic acids, anhydrides, esters, amides
- **Level 4** (four bonds to heteroatoms): carbon dioxide

Oxidation = loss of electrons, fewer bonds to hydrogens, more bonds to heteroatoms (O, N, halogens)

Reduction = gain of electrons, more bonds to hydrogens, fewer bonds to heteroatoms

Oxidizing Agents

Good oxidizing agents have a high affinity for electrons (such as O_2, O_3, and Cl_2) or unusually high oxidation states (like Mn^{7+} in permanganate, MnO_4^-, and Cr^{6+} in chromate, CrO_4^{2-}).

Reducing Agents

Good reducing agents include sodium, magnesium, aluminum, and zinc, which have low electronegativities and ionization energies. Metal hydrides are also good reducing agents, like NaH, CaH_2, $LiAlH_4$, and $NaBH_4$, because they contain the H^- ion.

Oxidation

- PCC takes a primary alcohol to an aldehyde.

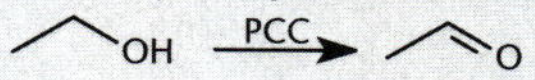

- Jones's reagent, $KMnO_4$, and alkali dichromate salts will convert secondary alcohols to ketones and primary alcohols to carboxylic acids.

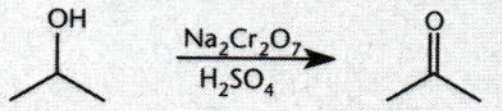

- Tertiary alcohols cannot be oxidized without breaking a carbon–carbon bond.

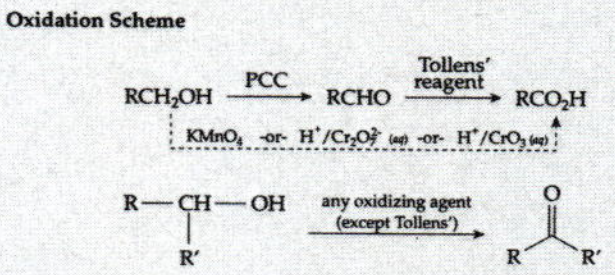

Reduction

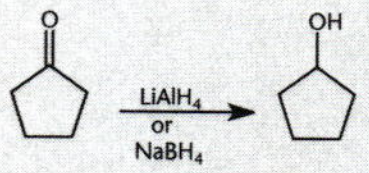

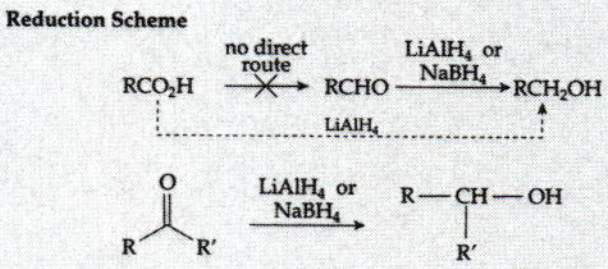

Alcohols and Reactivity

Alcohols can be converted to mesylates or tosylates to make them better leaving groups for nucleophilic substitution reactions.

- **Mesylates** ($-SO_3CH_3$) are derived from methanesulfonic acid.
- **Tosylates** ($-SO_3C_6H_4CH_3$) are derived from toluenesulfonic acid.

Alcohols can be used as **protecting groups** for carbonyls, as reaction with a dialcohol forms an unreactive acetal. After other reactions, the protecting group can be removed with aqueous acid.

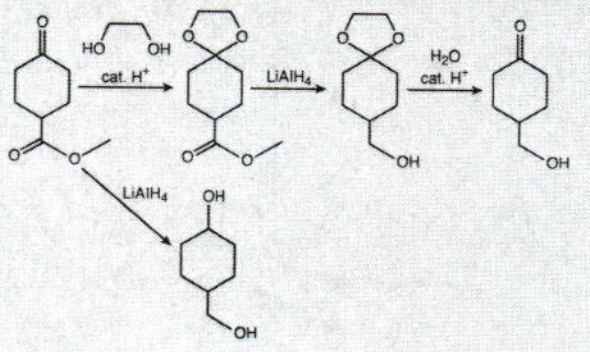

PHENOLS & QUINONE DERIVATIVES

The hydrogen of the hydroxyl group of a phenol is particularly acidic because the oxygen-containing anion is resonance-stabilized by the ring.

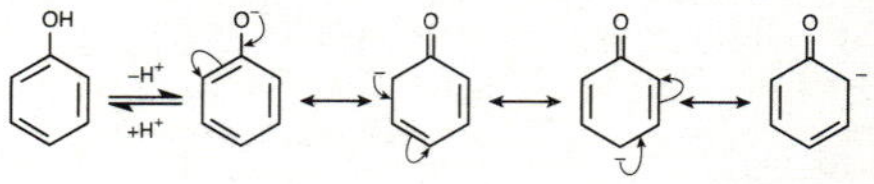

Quinones and Hydroxyquinones

Treatment of phenols with oxidizing agents produces **quinones**.

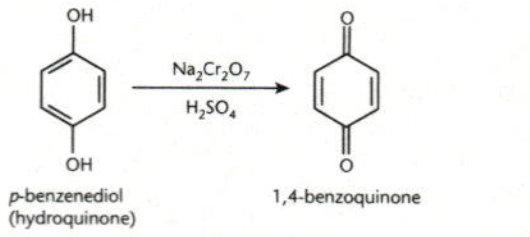

These molecules can be further oxidized to form a class of molecules called hydroxyquinones. Many hydroxyquinones have biological activity.

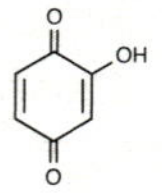

Ubiquinone

Ubiquinone is also called **coenzyme Q** and is a vital electron carrier associated with Complexes I, II, and III of the electron transport chain.

Ubiquinone can be reduced to **ubiquinol**, which can later be reoxidized to ubiquinone. This is sometimes called the **Q cycle**.

ALDEHYDES

The dipole moment of aldehydes causes an elevation of boiling point, but not as high as alcohols because there is no hydrogen bonding.

Synthesis

- Oxidation of primary alcohols
- Ozonolysis of alkenes

Reactions

Reactions of enols (Michael additions)

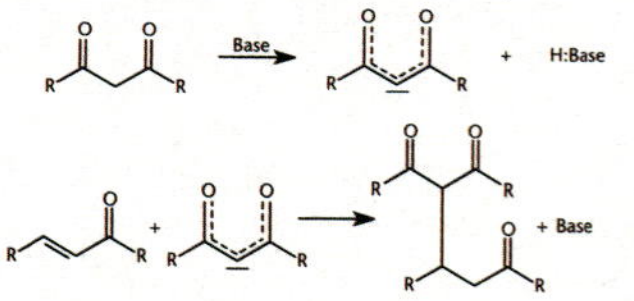

Nucleophilic addition to a carbonyl

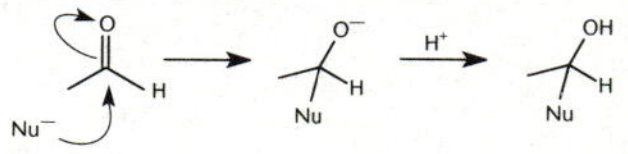

Aldol condensation

An aldehyde acts both as nucleophile (enol form) and electrophile (keto form). One carbonyl forms an enolate, which attacks the other carbonyl. After the aldol is formed, a dehydration reaction results in an α,β-unsaturated carbonyl.

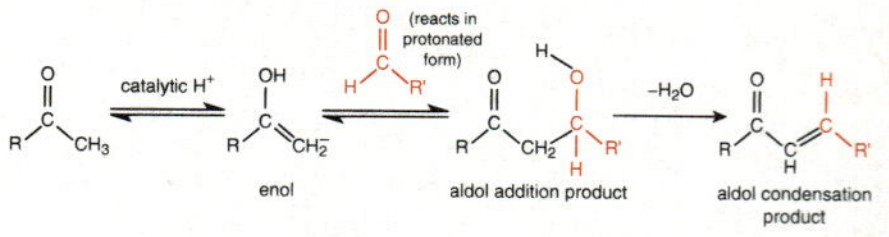

Decarboxylation

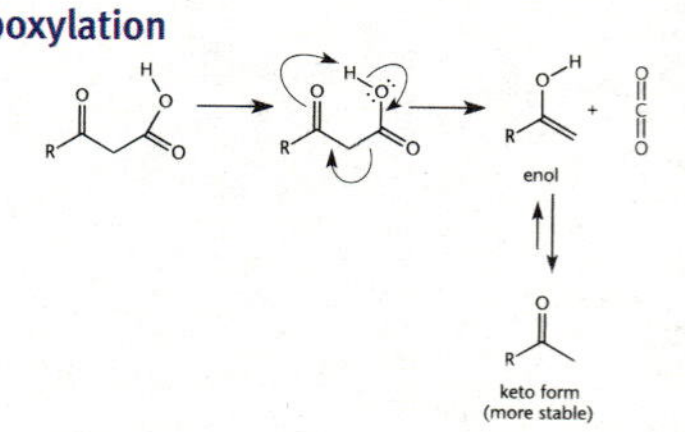

CARBOXYLIC ACIDS

Carboxylic acids have pK_a values around 4.5 due to resonance stabilization of the conjugate base. Electronegative atoms increase acidity with inductive effects. Boiling point is higher than alcohols because of the ability to form two hydrogen bonds.

Synthesis

Oxidation of primary alcohols with $KMnO_4$

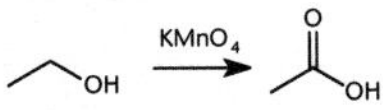

Reactions

Formation of soap by reacting carboxylic acids with NaOH; arrange in micelles

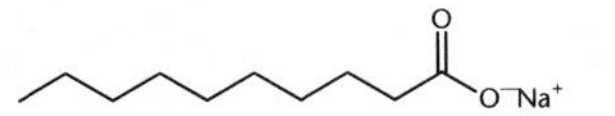

Nucleophilic acyl substitution

- General mechanism

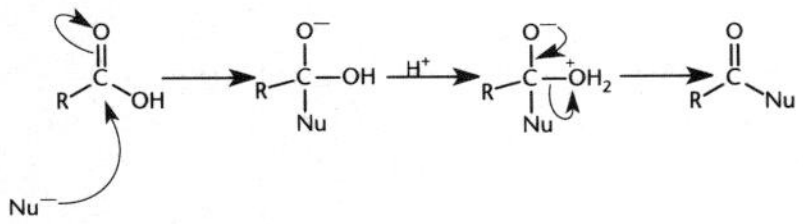

- Reduction to alcohols

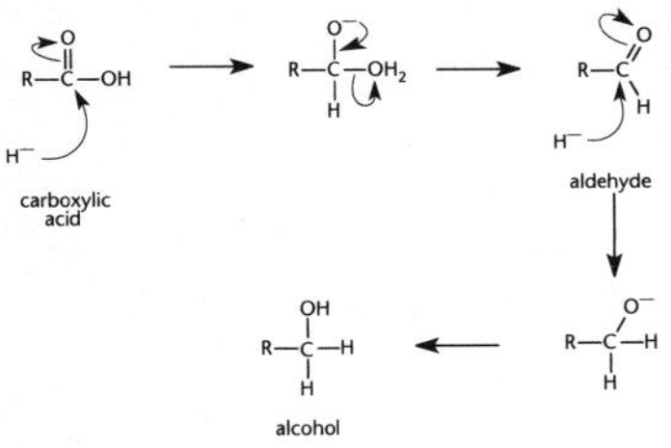

Decarboxylation

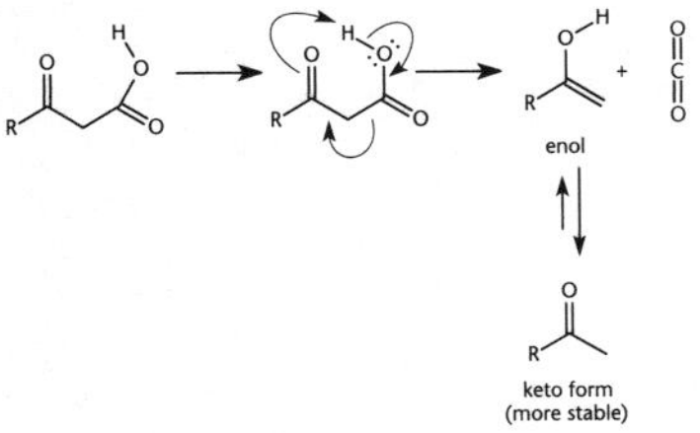

CYCLIC CARBOXYLIC ACID DERIVATIVES

Lactams

Cyclic amides are called **lactams**. These are named according to the carbon atom bonded to the nitrogen: β-lactams contain a bond between the β-carbon and the nitrogen, γ-lactams contain a bond between the γ-carbon and the nitrogen, and so forth.

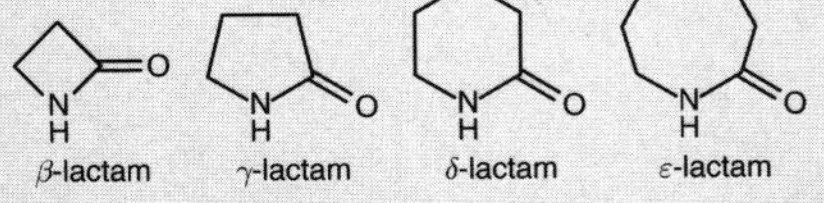

Lactones

Cyclic esters are called **lactones**. These are named not only based on the carbon bonded to the oxygen, but also the length of the carbon chain itself.

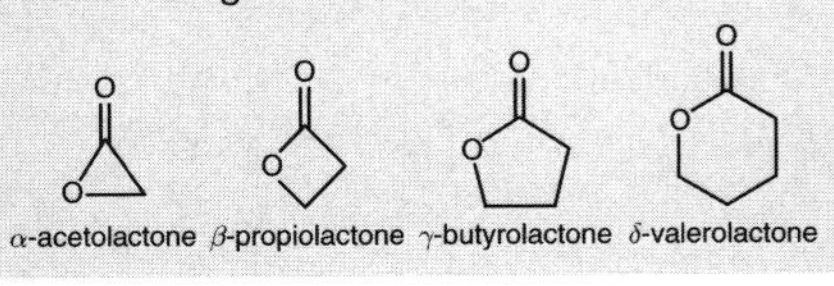

CARBOXYLIC ACID DERIVATIVES

Carboxylic acid derivatives contain three bonds to heteroatoms (O, N, halides, and so forth). As such, they can be interconverted through nucleophilic acyl substitution by swapping leaving groups.

Carboxylic acid derivatives can be ranked based on descending reactivity:

- Acyl halides are the most reactive
- Anhydrides
- Carboxylic acids and esters
- Amides are the least reactive

A reaction that proceeds down the order of reactivity can occur spontaneously by nucleophilic acyl substitution.

A reaction that proceeds up the order of reactivity requires special catalysts and specific reaction conditions.

Anhydrides

Synthesis via dehydration of two carboxylic acids

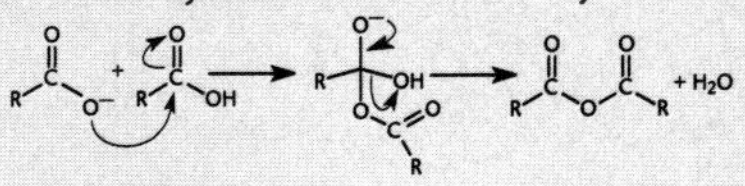

Intramolecular formation of a cyclic anhydride

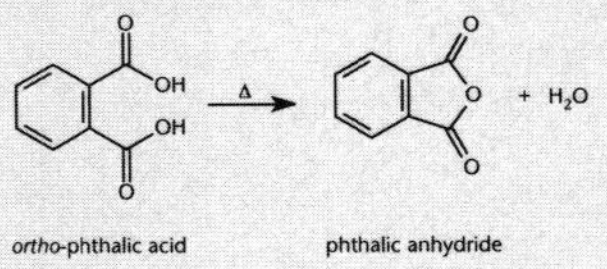

Amides

Formation from an anhydride

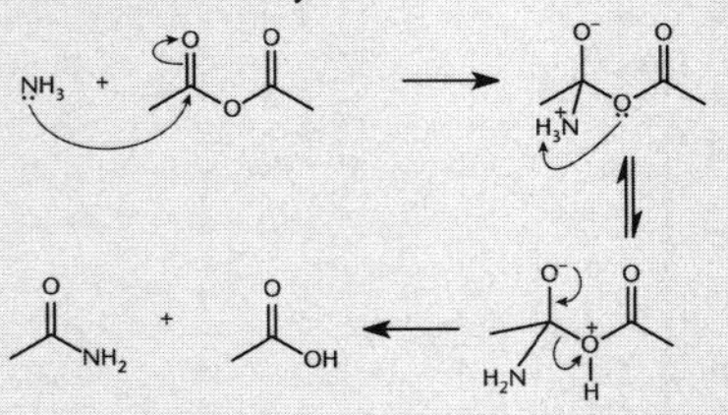

Formation from an ester

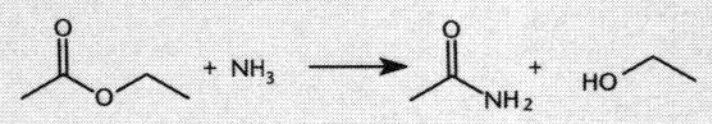

Hydrolysis (requires acid)

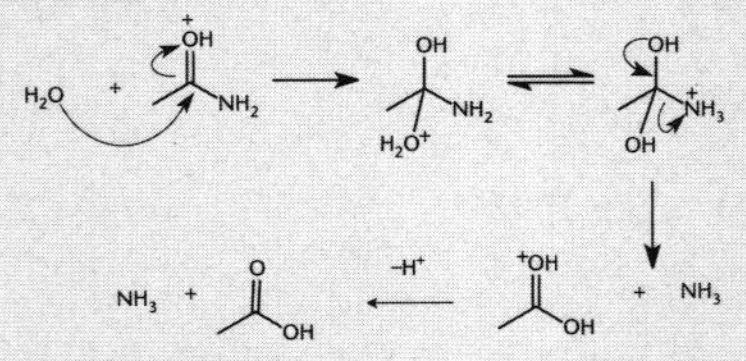

Reduction to an amine

Esters

Transesterification

Hydrolysis

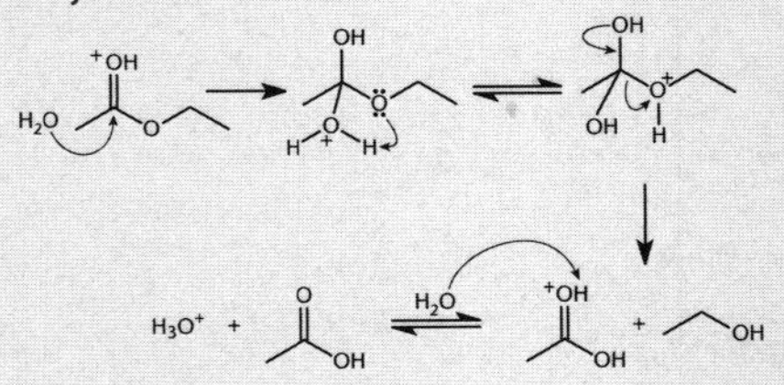

Reduction

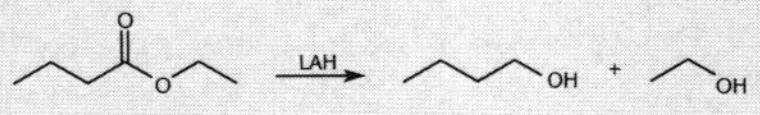

Saponification

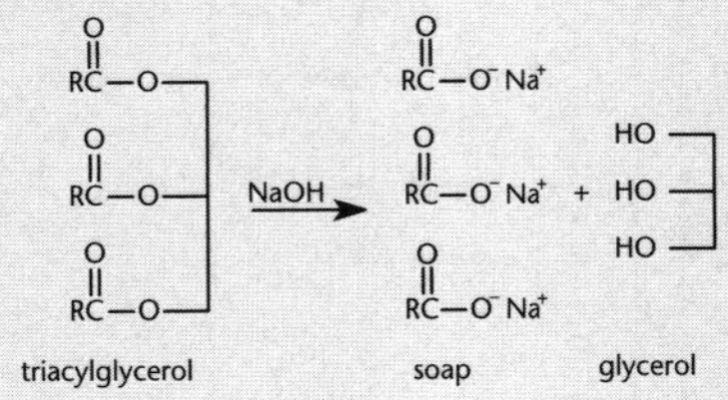

NITROGEN-CONTAINING COMPOUNDS

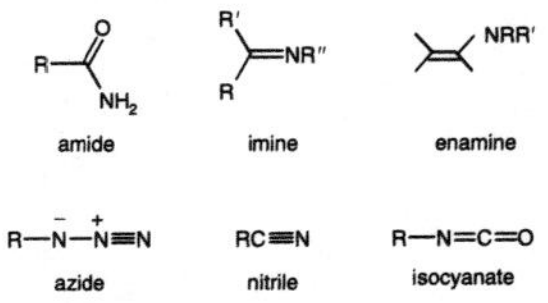

Strecker Synthesis

Reagents: aldehyde, ammonium chloride (NH_4Cl), potassium cyanide (KCN)

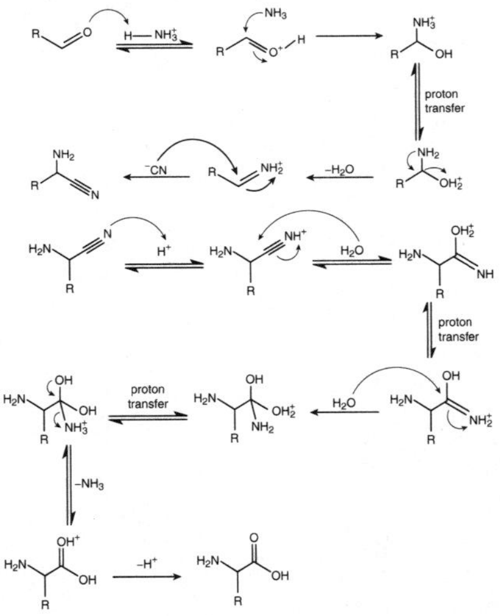

Gabriel (Malonic-Ester) Synthesis

Reagents: potassium phthalimide, diethyl bromomalonate

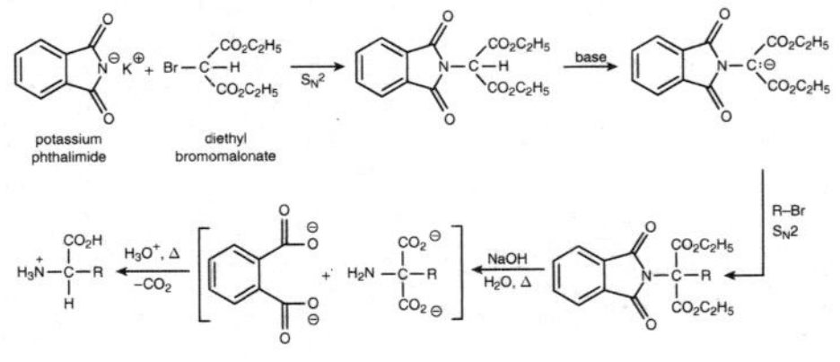

PHOSPHORUS-CONTAINING COMPOUNDS

- **Phosphoric acid** is a **phosphate group** or **inorganic phosphate (P_i)**. At physiologic pH, inorganic phosphate includes both hydrogen phosphate (HPO_4^{2-}) and dihydrogen phosphate ($H_2PO_4^-$).
- **Pyrophosphate (PP_i)** is $P_2O_7^{4-}$, which is released during the formation of phosphodiester bonds in DNA. Pyrophosphate is unstable in aqueous solution, and is hydrolyzed to form two molecules of inorganic phosphate.

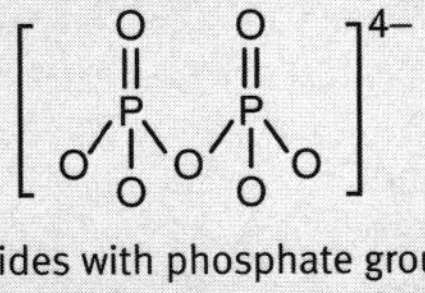

- Nucleotides with phosphate groups, such ATP, GTP, and those in DNA, are referred to as **organic phosphates**.

PURIFICATION METHODS

Extraction separates dissolved substances based on differential solubility in aqueous *vs.* organic solvents.

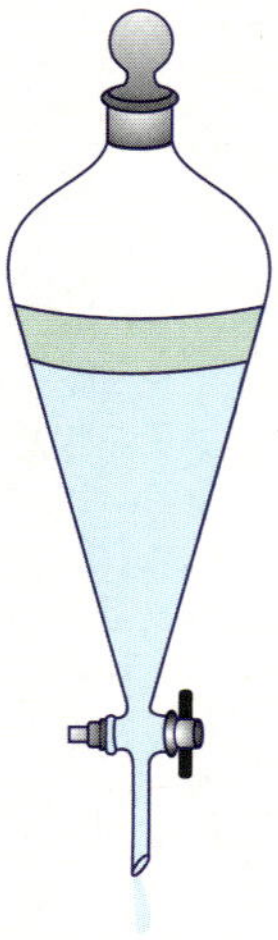

Filtration separates solids from liquids.

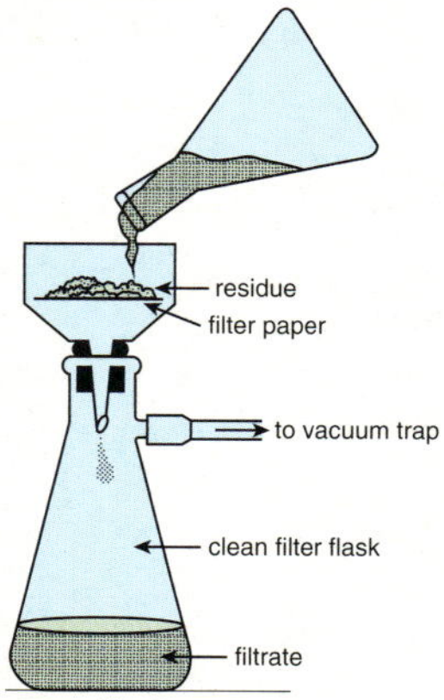

vacuum filtration

Chromatography uses a stationary phase and a mobile phase to separate compounds based on polarity and/or size.

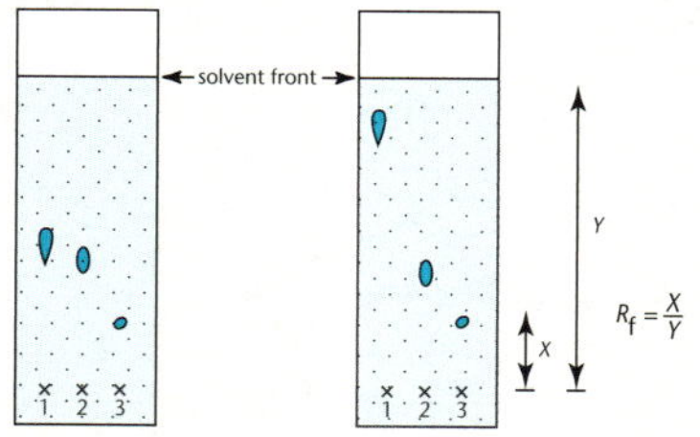

thin-layer chromatograms

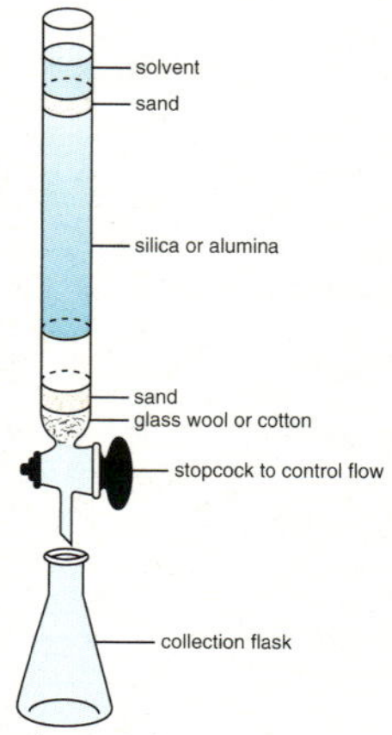

column chromatography

Distillation separates liquids based on boiling point, which depends on intermolecular forces. Types are simple, fractional, and vacuum.

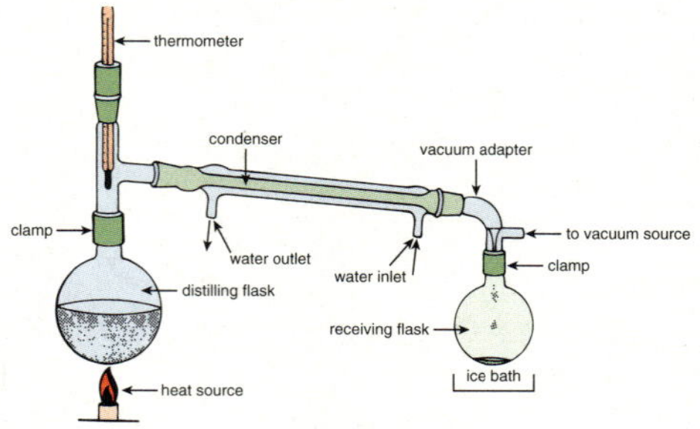

vacuum distillation

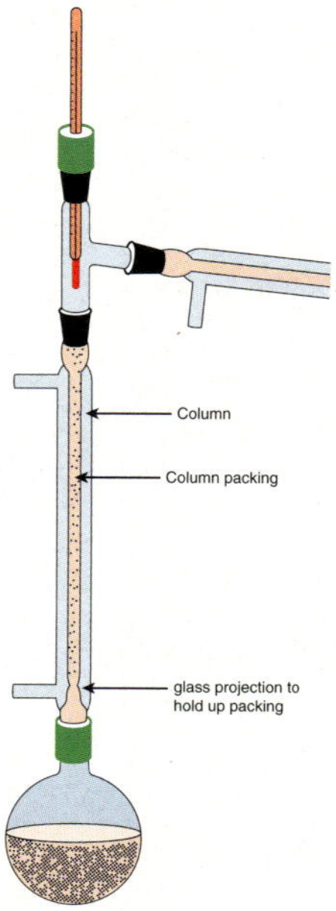

fractional distillation

Simple distillation can be used to separate two liquids with boiling points below 150°C and at least 25°C apart.

Vacuum distillation should be used when a liquid to be distilled has a boiling point above 150°C. To prevent degradation of the product, the incident pressure is lowered, thereby lowering the boiling point.

Fractional distillation should be used when two liquids have boiling points less than 25°C apart. By introducing a fractionation column, the sample boils and refluxes back down over a larger surface area, improving the purity of the distillate.

Recrystallization separates solids based on differential solubility in varying temperatures.

Electrophoresis is used to separate biological macromolecules based on size and/or charge.

SPECTROSCOPY

Infrared spectroscopy measures molecular vibrations of characteristic functional groups.

Functional Group	Wavenumber (cm^{-1})	Vibration
Alkanes	2800 — 3000	C—H
	1200	C—C
Alkenes	3080 — 3140	=C—H
	1645	C=C
Alkynes	2200	C≡C
	3300	≡C—H
Aromatic	2900 — 3100	C—H
	1475 — 1625	C—C
Alcohols	3100 — 3500	O—H (broad)
Ethers	1050 — 1150	C—O
Aldehydes	2700 — 2900	(O)C—H
	1700 — 1750	C=O
Ketones	1700 — 1750	C=O
Carboxylic acids	1700 — 1750	C=O
	2800 — 3200	O—H (broad)
Amines	3100 — 3500	N—H (sharp)

UV spectroscopy involves passing ultraviolet light through a chemical sample and plotting absorbance *vs.* wavelength. It is most useful for studying compounds containing double bonds and heteroatoms with lone pairs.

^{1}H–NMR is a form of **nuclear magnetic resonance.**

Type of Proton	Approximate Chemical Shift δ (ppm) Downfield from TMS
RCH_3	0.9
RCH_2	1.25
R_3CH	1.5
–CH=CH	4.6–6
–C≡CH	2–3
Ar–H	6–8.5
–CHX	2–4.5
–CHOH/–CHOR	3.4–4
RCHO	9–10
RCHCO–	2–2.5
–CHCOOH/–CHCOOR	2–2.6
–CHOH–CH_2OH	1–5.5
ArOH	4–12
–COOH	10.5–12
–NH_2	1–5

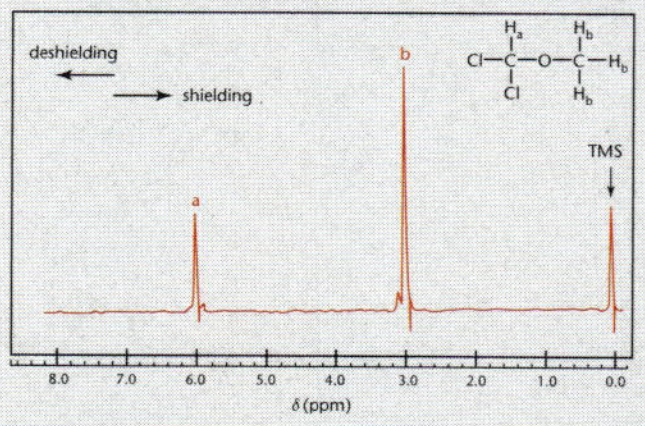

When analyzing an NMR spectrum, look for:

- **Types of protons:** corresponds to the number of peaks seen in the spectrum
- **Position of peaks:** the further left-shifted (downfield) the peak, the more deshielded the proton. Usually this corresponds to more electron-withdrawing groups
- **Integration of peaks:** the larger the integration, the more protons contained under the peak
- **Splitting:** hydrogens on adjacent carbons will split a peak into $n + 1$ subpeaks, where n is the number of hydrogens on the adjacent carbon

Type of Chromatography	Mobile Phase	Stationary Phase	Common Use
Thin-layer or Paper	Nonpolar solvent	Polar card	Identify a sample
Reverse-phase	Polar solvent	Nonpolar card	Identify a sample
Column	Nonpolar solvent	Polar gel or powder	Separate a sample into components
Ion-exchange	Nonpolar solvent	Charged beads in column	Separate components by charge
Size-exclusion	Nonpolar solvent	Polar, porous beads in column	Separate components by size
Affinity	Nonpolar solvent	Beads coated with antibody or receptor for a target molecule	Purify a molecule (usually a protein) of interest
Gas (GC)	Inert gas	Crushed metal or polymer	Separate vaporizable compounds
High-performance liquid (HPLC)	Nonpolar solvent	Small column with concentration gradient	Similar to column, but more precise

KINEMATICS

Vectors: physical quantities with both magnitude and direction

- Examples: force, velocity

Scalars: physical quantities that have magnitude, but no direction

- Examples: mass, speed

Displacement ($\Delta\mathbf{x}$): the change in position that goes in a straight-line path from the initial position to the final position; independent of the path taken (SI unit: m)

Average velocity: $\bar{\mathbf{v}} = \frac{\Delta \mathbf{x}}{\Delta t}$ (SI units: $\frac{m}{s}$)

Acceleration: the rate of change of an object's velocity; it is a vector quantity: $\mathbf{a} = \frac{\Delta \mathbf{v}}{\Delta t}$ (SI units: $\frac{m}{s^2}$)

Linear Motion

$\mathbf{v} = \mathbf{v}_0 + \mathbf{a}t$

$\mathbf{x} = \mathbf{v}_0 t + \frac{1}{2}\mathbf{a}t^2$

$\mathbf{v}^2 = \mathbf{v}_0^2 + 2\mathbf{ax}$

$\bar{\mathbf{v}} = \frac{(\mathbf{v}_0 + \mathbf{v})}{2}$

$\mathbf{x} = \bar{\mathbf{v}}t = \left(\frac{(\mathbf{v}_0 + \mathbf{v})}{2}\right)t$

- When solving for time, there will be two values for t: when the projectile is initially launched and when it impacts the ground.
- To find max height, remember that the vertical velocity of the projectile is 0 at the highest point of the path.

Projectile Motion

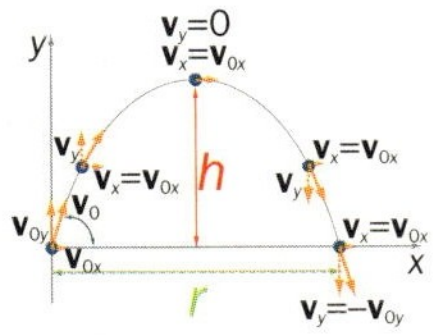

- Vertical component of velocity = $v \sin \theta$
- Horizontal component of velocity = $v \cos \theta$

Frictional forces

Static friction (f_s): is the force that must be overcome to set an object in motion. It has the formula: $0 \le f_s \le \mu_s N$

Kinetic friction (f_k): opposes the motion of objects moving relative to each other. It has the formula: $f_k = \mu_k N$

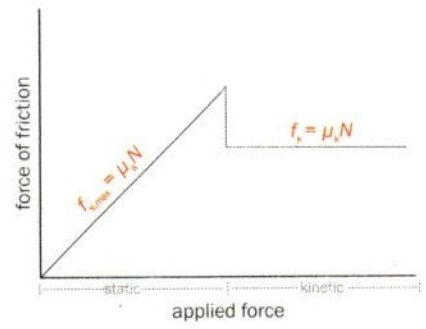

Newton's first law (law of inertia): A body in a state of motion or at rest will remain in that state unless acted upon by a net force.

Newton's second law: When a net force is applied to a body of mass m, the body will be accelerated in the same direction as the force applied to the mass. This is expressed by the formula $\mathbf{F} = m\mathbf{a}$ [SI unit: newton (N) = $\frac{kg \cdot m}{s^2}$].

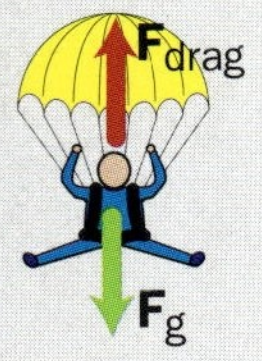

- $F_{gravity} > F_{drag}$: person accelerates downward
- $F_g = F_{drag}$: terminal velocity is reached (person travels at constant velocity)

WORK AND ENERGY

Work: For a constant force **F** acting on an object that moves a displacement of **d**, the work is $W = Fd \cos \theta$. (For a force perpendicular to the displacement, $W = 0$.) [SI unit: joule = N·m]

System Work

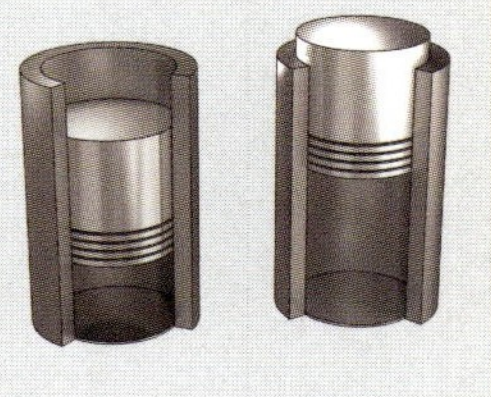

- When the piston expands, work is done *by* the system ($W > 0$).
- When the piston compresses the gas, work is done *on* the system ($W < 0$).
- The area under a P vs. V curve is the amount of work done in a system.

Power: the rate at which work is performed; it is given by: $P = \frac{W}{\Delta t}$ (SI unit: watt = $\frac{J}{s}$)

Mechanical Energy

Energy is a scalar quantity (SI unit: joule).

Kinetic energy: the energy associated with moving objects. It is given by:

$$K = \frac{1}{2}mv^2$$

Potential energy: the energy associated with a body's position. Gravitational potential energy of an object is due to the force of gravity acting on it and is expressed as: $U = mgh$

Total mechanical energy

$$E = U + K$$

Mechanical energy is conserved when the sum of kinetic and potential energies remains constant.

Work–Energy Theorem

Relates the work performed by all forces acting on a body in a particular time interval to the change in energy at that time:

$$W = \Delta E$$

Conservation of Energy

When there are no nonconservative forces (such as friction) acting on a system, the total mechanical energy remains constant: $\Delta E = \Delta K + \Delta U = 0$

NEWTON'S LAWS

Newton's third law: If body A exerts a force on body B, then B will exert a force back onto A that is equal in magnitude, but opposite in direction. This can be expressed as $\mathbf{F}_b = -\mathbf{F}_a$.

Newton's law of gravitation: All forms of matter experience an attractive force to other forms of matter in the universe. The magnitude of the force is represented by: $F = \frac{Gm_1 m_2}{r^2}$

- **Mass (m):** a scalar quantity that measures a body's inertia
- **Weight ($\mathbf{F}_g$):** a vector quantity that measures a body's gravitational attraction to the earth ($\mathbf{F}_g = m\mathbf{g}$)

Uniform circular motion:

$a_c = \frac{v^2}{r}$

$F_c = \frac{mv^2}{r}$

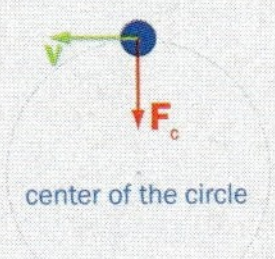

Equilibrium

First condition of equilibrium: An object is in translational equilibrium when the sum of forces pushing it one direction is counterbalanced by the sum of forces acting in the opposite direction. It can be expressed as $\Sigma\mathbf{F} = 0$.

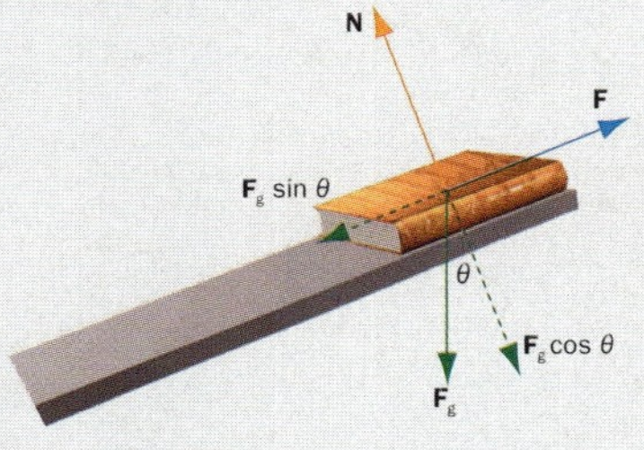

Problem-Solving Guide

- Resolve the forces into x- and y-components.
- $\Sigma\mathbf{F} = 0$ must be true for equilibrium; therefore, $\Sigma\mathbf{F}_x = 0$ and $\Sigma\mathbf{F}_y = 0$.

THERMODYNAMICS

Thermal Expansion

Linear expansion: the increase in length by most solids when heated

Mnemonic: when temperature increases, the length of a solid increases "a Lot"($\alpha L \Delta T$)

$$\Delta L = \alpha L \Delta T$$

Volume expansion: the increase in volume of fluids when heated

$$\Delta V = \beta V \Delta T$$

Heat Transfer

Conduction: the direct transfer of energy via molecular collisions

Convection: the transfer of heat by the physical motion of a fluid

Radiation: the transfer of energy by electromagnetic waves

Specific Heat

$Q = mc\Delta T$ (mnemonic: looks like MCAT)

- Can only be used to find Q when the object does not change phase
- $Q > 0$ means heat is gained; $Q < 0$ means heat is lost

[Common units: joules, calories, or Calories (kcal)]

Heat of transformation: the quantity of heat required to change the phase of 1 g of a substance.

$Q = mL$ (phase changes are isothermal processes)

First law of thermodynamics: $\Delta U = Q - W$

Process	First Law Becomes
Adiabatic ($Q = 0$)	$\Delta U = -W$
Constant volume ($W = 0$)	$\Delta U = Q$
Isothermal ($\Delta U = 0$)	$Q = W$

Second law of thermodynamics: In any thermodynamic process that moves from one state of equilibrium to another, the entropy of the system and environment together will either increase or remain unchanged.

HYDROSTATICS & FLUID DYNAMICS

Density (ρ) = $\frac{m}{V}$ [SI units: $\frac{kg}{m^3}$]

Specific gravity = $\frac{\rho_{subtance}}{\rho_{water}}$ [no units]; $\rho_{water} = 10^3\ \frac{kg}{m^3}$

Weight = $\rho g V$

Pressure: a scalar quantity defined as force per unit area: $P = \frac{F}{A}$ [SI units: pascal = $\frac{N}{m^2}$]

- For static fluids of uniform density in a sealed vessel, pressure: $P = \rho gz$
- **Absolute pressure** in a fluid due to gravity somewhere below the surface is given by the equation $P = P_o + \rho gz$
- **Gauge pressure:** $P_g = P - P_{atm}$

Continuity equation: $A_1v_1 = A_2v_2$

Bernoulli's equation: $P + \frac{1}{2}\rho v^2 + \rho gh$ = constant

Archimedes' Principle

$F_{buoy} = \rho_{fluid}\, gV_{submerged}$

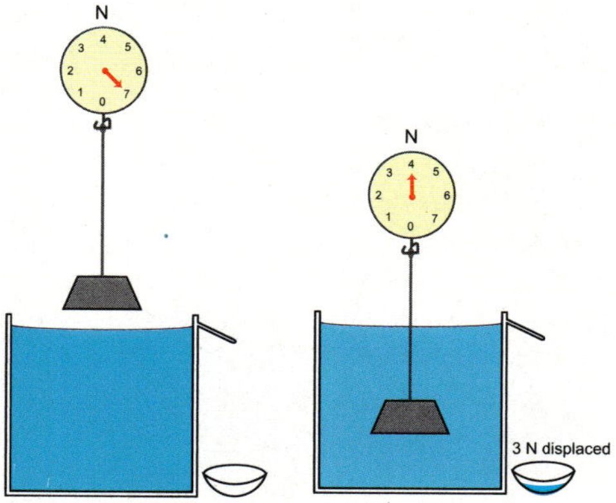

- The buoyant force is equal to the weight of the displaced fluid.
  - If the weight of the fluid displaced is less than the object's weight, the object will sink.
  - If the weight of the fluid displaced is greater than or equal to the object's weight, then it will float.

Pascal's Principle

- A change in the pressure applied to an enclosed fluid is transmitted undiminished to every portion of the fluid and to the walls of the containing vessel.

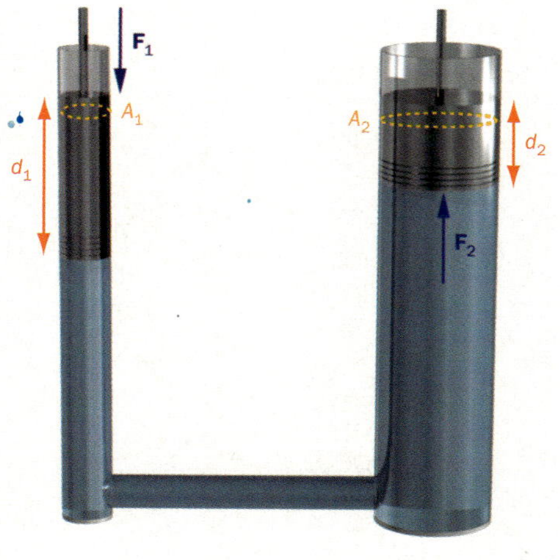

$$P = \frac{F_1}{A_1} = \frac{F_2}{A_2} \text{ and } A_1d_1 = A_2d_2$$

so, $W = F_1d_1 = F_2d_2$

ELECTROSTATICS

Coulomb's Law

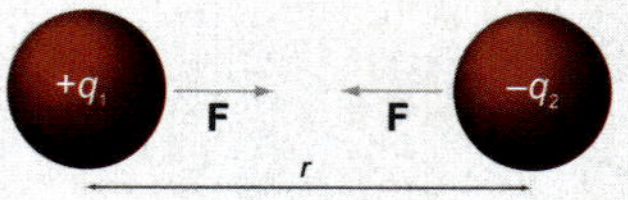

$$F = \frac{kq_1q_2}{r^2} \text{ [SI units: newton]}$$

Electric Field

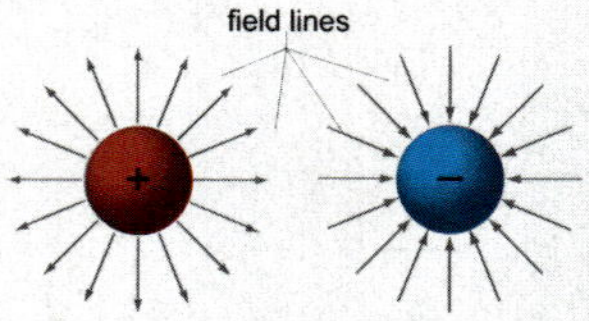

$$E = \frac{F_e}{q} = \frac{kQ}{r^2} \text{ [SI units: } \frac{N}{C} \text{ or } \frac{V}{m}]$$

- A positive point charge will move in the same direction as the electric field vector; a negative charge will move in the opposite direction.

Electrical Potential Energy (*U*)

The electrical potential energy of a charge *q* at a point in space is the amount of work required to move it from infinity to that point.

$$U = q\Delta V = qEd = \frac{kQq}{r} \text{ [SI units: J]}$$

Electric Dipoles

- **p** is the dipole moment (**p** = *q***d**).
- The dipole feels no net translational force, but experiences a torque about the center causing it to rotate so that the dipole moment aligns with the electric field.

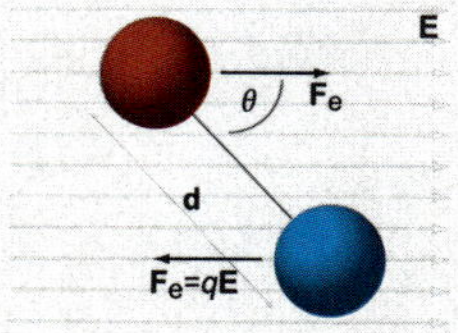

Electrical Potential

The amount of work required to move a positive test charge *q* from infinity to a particular point divided by the test charge: $V = \frac{U}{q}$ [SI units: volt = $\frac{J}{C}$]

Potential Difference (Voltage)

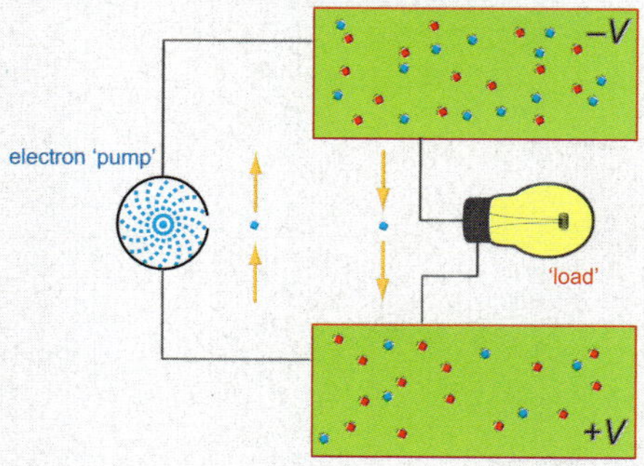

$$\text{Voltage } (\Delta V) = \frac{W}{q} = \frac{kQ}{r} \text{ [SI units: volt} = \frac{J}{C}]$$

- When two oppositely charged parallel plates are separated by a distance *d*, an electric field is created, and a potential difference exists between the plates, given by: $V = Ed$

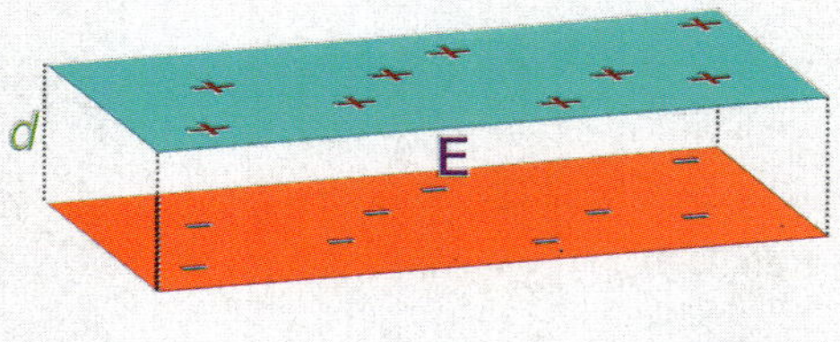

CIRCUITS

Current: the flow of electric charge. Current is given by:

$$I = \frac{Q}{\Delta t} \text{ [SI units: ampère (A)} = \frac{C}{s}]$$

(The direction of current is the direction positive charge would flow, or from high to low potential.)

Ohm's Law and Resistance

$V = IR$ (can be applied to entire circuit or individual resistors)

Resistance: opposition to the flow of charge. $R = \frac{\rho L}{A}$ (Resistance increases with increasing temperatures for most materials.)

[SI Units: ohm (Ω)]

Circuit Laws

Kirchhoff's laws:

1. At any junction within a circuit, the sum of current flowing into that point must equal the sum of current leaving.
2. The sum of voltage sources equals the sum of voltage drops around a closed-circuit loop.

Series Circuits

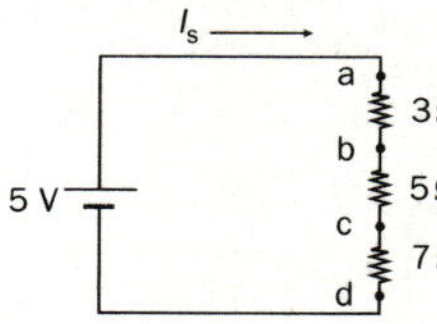

$R_{eq} = R_1 + R_2 + R_3 + ...$
$V_T = V_1 + V_2 + V_3 + ...$
$I_T = I_1 = I_2 = I_3 = ...$

Parallel Circuits

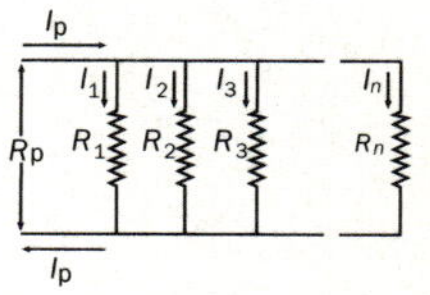

$\frac{1}{R_{eq}} = \frac{1}{R_1} + \frac{1}{R_2} + \frac{1}{R_3} + ...$
$V_T = V_1 = V_2 = V_3 = ...$
$I_T = I_1 + I_2 + I_3 + ...$

Power Dissipated by Resistors

$$P = IV = \frac{V^2}{R} = I^2R$$

Capacitors

Capacitance: the ability to store charge per unit voltage. It is given by: $C = \frac{Q}{V}$

$$C' = \kappa\frac{\varepsilon_0 A}{d}$$

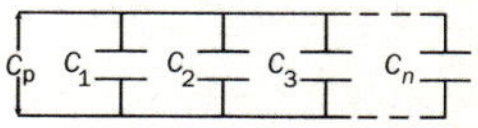

Capacitors in parallel: add
$C_{eq} = C_1 + C_2 + C_3 + ...$

Capacitors in series: add as reciprocals, then take reciprocal of sum
$\frac{1}{C_{eq}} = \frac{1}{C_1} + \frac{1}{C_2} + \frac{1}{C_3} + ...$

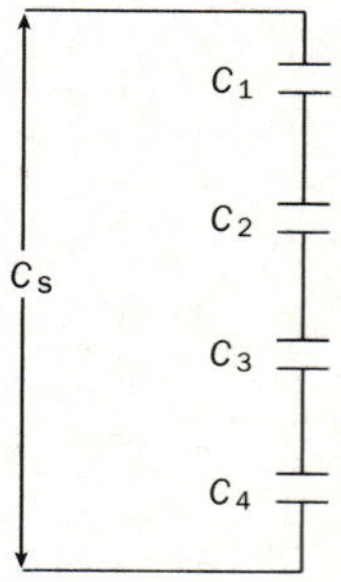

Energy Stored by Capacitors

$$U = \frac{1}{2}QV = \frac{1}{2}CV^2 = \frac{1}{2}\frac{Q^2}{C}$$

WAVES

Describing Waves

Longitudinal wave

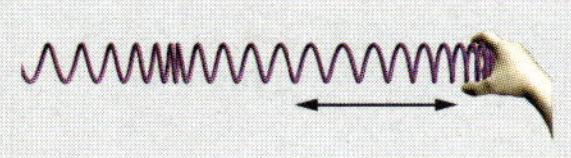

Transverse wave

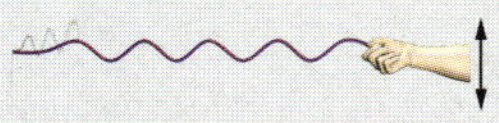

Wave formulas

$$f = \frac{1}{T}$$

$$v = f\lambda$$

Standing Waves

Strings

$\lambda = \frac{2L}{n}$ $(n = 1, 2, 3\ldots)$

$f = \frac{nv}{2L}$ $(n = 1, 2, 3\ldots)$

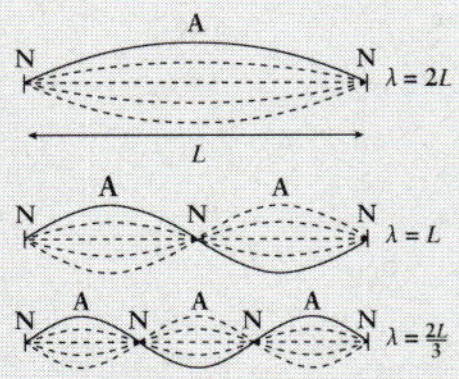

The ends of the strings are always nodes. Nodes occur where the displacement is zero.

Open pipes

$\lambda = \frac{2L}{n}$ $(n = 1, 2, 3\ldots)$

$f = \frac{nv}{2L}$ $(n = 1, 2, 3\ldots)$

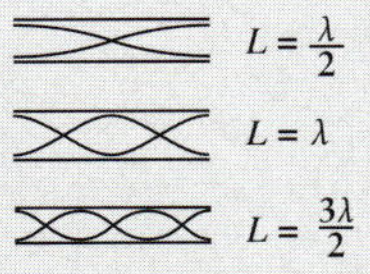

The open ends of the pipes are always antinodes (max amplitude).

Closed pipes

$\lambda = \frac{4L}{n}$ $(n = 1, 3, 5\ldots)$

$f = \frac{nv}{4L}$ $(n = 1, 3, 5\ldots)$

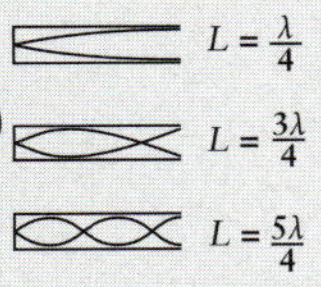

The closed end of the pipe is always a node, and the open end is always an antinode.

SOUND

Sound propagates through a deformable medium by the oscillation of particles parallel to the direction of the wave's propagation.

Intensity (I) = $\frac{P}{A}$ [SI units: $\frac{W}{m^2}$]

Sound level (β) = $10 \log \left(\frac{I}{I_0}\right)$ [unit: decibel = dB]

(Note than an increase of 10 dB is an increase in intensity by a factor of 10. An increase of 20 dB is an increase in intensity by a factor of 100.)

Doppler Effect

- When a source and a detector move relative to one another, the perceived frequency of the sound received differs from the actual frequency emitted.

$$f' = f\frac{(v \pm v_D)}{(v \mp v_S)}$$

Stationary source: $v_S = 0$

Stationary detector: $v_D = 0$

Observer and detector moving closer:

- + sign in numerator
- − sign in denominator

Observer and detector moving apart:

- − sign in numerator
- + sign in denominator

OPTICS

Refraction

$n = \frac{c}{v}$ (speed of light = $3 \times 10^8 \frac{m}{s}$)

Snell's law: $n_1 \sin\theta_1 = n_2 \sin\theta_2$. When $n_2 > n_1$, light bends toward the normal; when $n_2 < n_1$, light bends away from the normal.

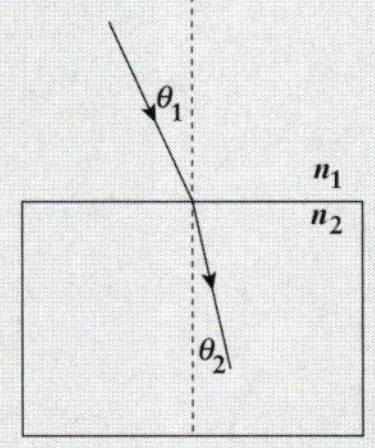

Diffraction

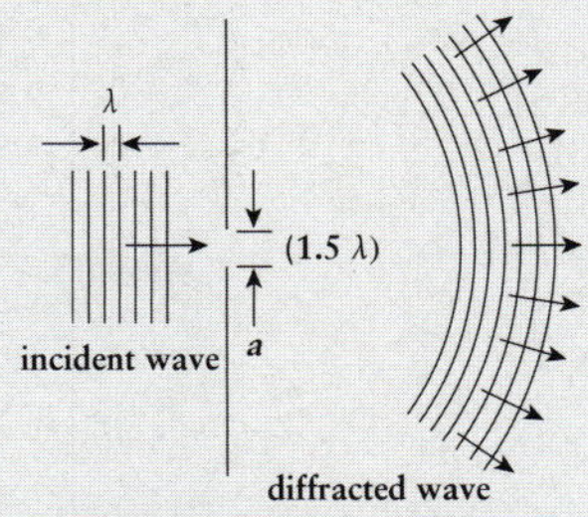

To locate dark fringes, use the formula:

$$a \sin\theta = n\lambda \ (n = 1, 2, 3\ldots)$$

Spherical Mirrors

Optics equation: $\frac{1}{o} + \frac{1}{i} = \frac{1}{f} = \frac{2}{r}$

- Any of units of distance may be used, but all units used must be the same.

Concave mirrors

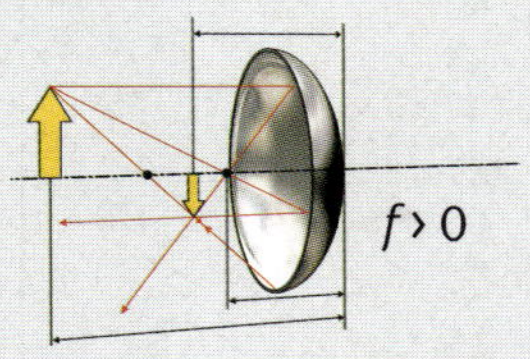

- If an object is placed inside the focal length of a concave mirror instead, the image formed is behind the mirror, enlarged and virtual.

Convex mirrors

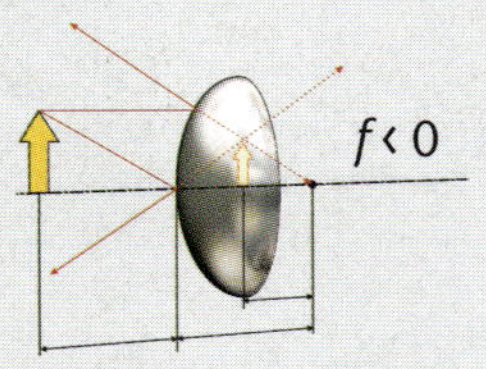

- Regardless of the position of the object, a convex mirror forms only a virtual upright image.

Thin Spherical Lenses

Optics equation: $\frac{1}{f} = \frac{1}{o} + \frac{1}{i}$

Converging lenses

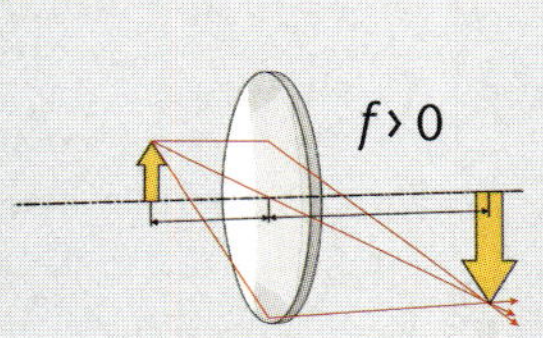

- For an object beyond the focal length, the image formed is real and inverted.
- For an object inside the focal length, the image formed is virtual, upright and enlarged.
- There is no image formed if an object is at the focal point.

Diverging lenses

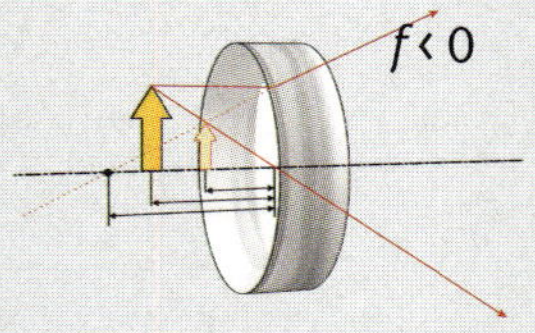

Magnification (m) = $\frac{-i}{o}$

- $|m| < 1$ image reduced; $|m| > 1$ image enlarged; $|m| = 1$ image same size
- Inverted image has a negative m; erect image has a positive m

ATOMIC AND NUCLEAR PHENOMENA

Photoelectric Effect

$E = hf = \frac{hc}{\lambda}$

$K = hf - W$

K is the maximum kinetic energy of an ejected electron; *W* is the minimum energy required to eject an electron, called the work function.

Nuclear Binding Energy

Mass defect: the difference between the sum of the masses of nucleons in the nucleus and the mass of the nucleus. The mass defect results from the conversion of matter to energy, embodied by: $E = mc^2$. This energy is the **binding energy** that holds nucleons within the nucleus.

Exponential Decay

Half-life

$n = n_0 e^{-\lambda t}$

Alpha decay

${}^{238}_{92}U \rightarrow {}^{234}_{90}Th + {}^{4}_{2}He$

Beta-minus decay

${}^{137}_{55}Cs \rightarrow {}^{137}_{56}Ba + {}^{0}_{-1}e^- + \bar{\nu}_e$

Beta-plus decay

${}^{22}_{11}Na \rightarrow {}^{22}_{10}Ne + {}^{0}_{+1}e^+ + \nu_e$

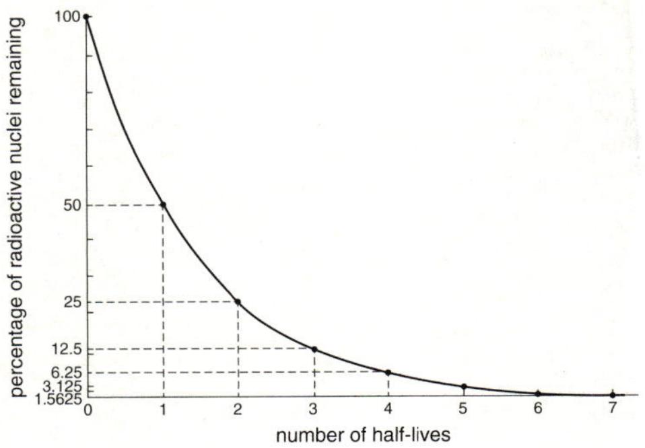

MATHEMATICS

Estimation

Scientific notation: A method of simplifying calculations by reducing numbers to a significand between one and ten and the exponent power of ten: $0.0000037 = 3.7 \times 10^{-6}$. Allows estimation by powers of ten, which is often all that is necessary on the MCAT.

Multiplication: If you round one number up, round the other down to compensate.

Division: If you round one number up, round the other up to compensate.

Roots and Logarithms

x	x^2	x	x^2	x	x^2	x	x^2
1	1	**6**	36	**11**	121	**16**	256
2	4	**7**	49	**12**	144	**17**	289
3	9	**8**	64	**13**	169	**18**	324
4	16	**9**	81	**14**	196	**19**	361
5	25	**10**	100	**15**	225	**20**	400

This table can be used to estimate even-powered roots of numbers. When taking square roots of a number raised to a power, remember not to take the square root of the exponent, but to divide it by two.

Logarithmic identities

$$\log A \times B = \log A + \log B$$

$$\log \frac{A}{B} = \log A - \log B$$

$$\log A^B = B \log A$$

$$\log \frac{1}{A} = -\log A$$

Converting common and natural logarithms

$$\log x = \frac{\ln x}{2.303}$$

$$\log (n \times 10^m) \approx m + 0.n$$

Trigonometry

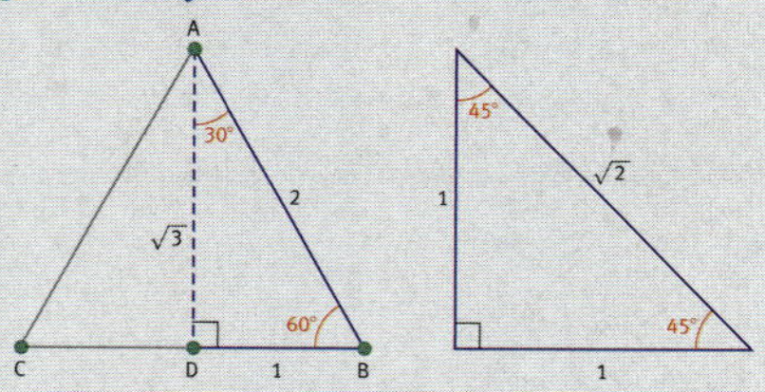

$$\sin\theta = \frac{\text{opposite}}{\text{hypotenuse}}$$

$$\cos\theta = \frac{\text{adjacent}}{\text{hypotenuse}}$$

$$\tan\theta = \frac{\text{opposite}}{\text{adjacent}}$$

Vector Addition and Subtraction

Tip-to-tail method of finding resultant of two vectors:

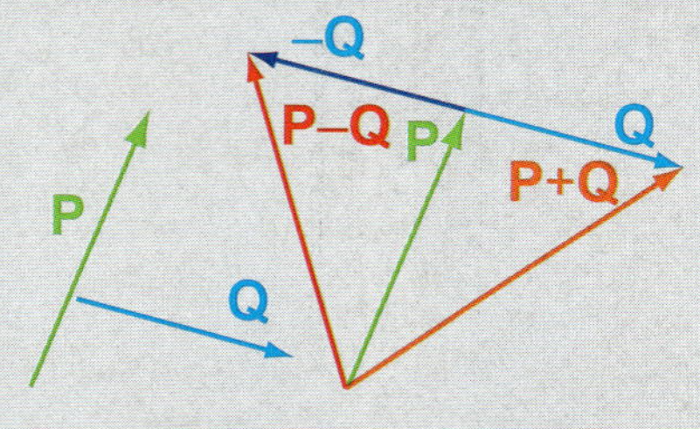

Finding the resultant using the component method:

- Resolve vectors into *x*- and *y*-components
- Sum all the vectors in the *x*-direction to get the resultant for the *x*-direction, and do the same for the *y*-components
- The magnitude of the resultant $R = \sqrt{R_x^2 + R_y^2}$

Right-Hand Rule for Finding Direction of Cross-Product Resultant

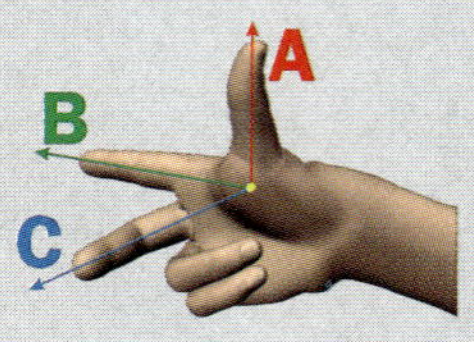

The right-hand rule is used to find the direction of a vector that is the product of two other vectors. If **C** = **A** × **B**, then **C** is represented by the palm while **A** is represented by the thumb and **B** is represented by the fingers.

RESEARCH DESIGN

Question Selection

Scientific method: determine whether sufficient background exists and whether the question is testable

FINER method: determine whether a study is **F**easible, **I**nteresting, **N**ovel, **E**thical, and **R**elevant

Causality

Controls: experimental subjects that are maintained with similar but noninterventional treatments to establish causality

Hill's criteria: help determine the strength of causal relationships. Only temporality is necessary.

Error Sources

- **Small sample size:** amplifies the effects of statistical anomalies
- **Defects in precision and accuracy:** create random or systematic variations in the data

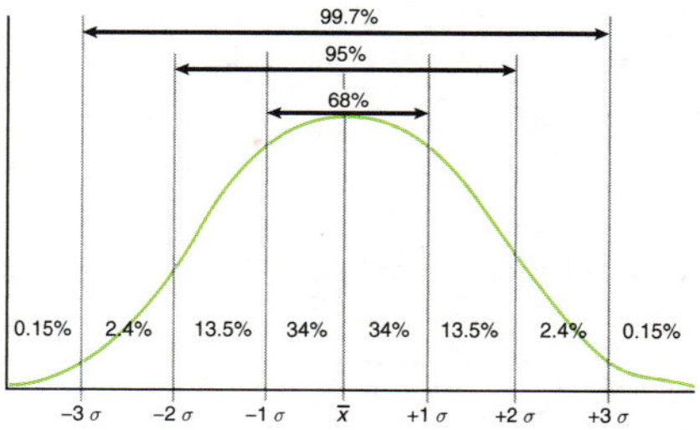

- **Bias:** systematic data error. Common types include **selection bias, detection bias,** and the **Hawthorne effect**. Minimized by proper participant selection, blinding, and randomization.
- **Confounding:** an analysis error wherein a variable that has a relationship with the other two variables is overlooked

Ethics

- **Beneficence:** the requirement to do good
- **Nonmaleficence:** "do no harm"
- **Autonomy:** the right of individuals to make decisions for themselves
- **Justice:** the need to consider only morally relevant differences between patients and to distribute healthcare resources fairly

Generalizability

Statistical significance and causality do not make something generalizable or a good intervention. **Clinical significance** and the **target population** must also be considered.

DATA ANALYSIS

Measures of Central Tendency and Distribution

- **Mean:** the average of the data points; impacted heavily by outliers
- **Median:** the central value of a data set; not affected by outliers
- **Mode:** the most common data point(s); not affected by outliers
- **Range:** the difference between the largest and smallest value in a set; impacted heavily by outliers
- **Standard deviation:** a measure of how spread out values are from the mean; affected by outliers

$$\sigma = \sqrt{\frac{\sum_{i=1}^{n}\left(x_i - \bar{x}\right)^2}{n-1}}$$

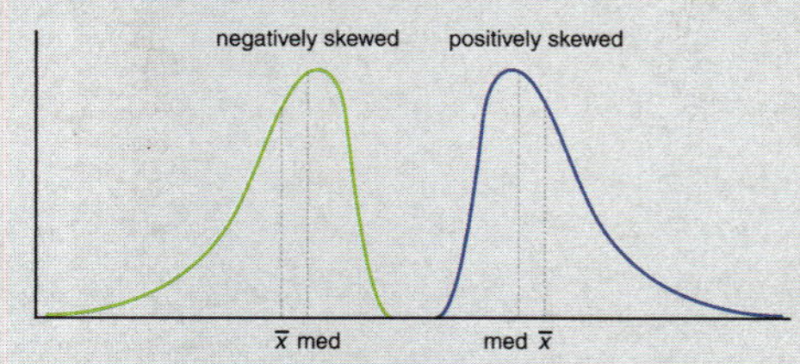

Probability

- **Mutually exclusive:** two events that cannot occur together
- **Independent:** the probability of either event is not affected by the occurrence of the other

For independent events:

$$P(\text{A and B}) = P(\text{A}) \times P(\text{B})$$

$$P(\text{A or B}) = P(\text{A}) + P(\text{B}) - P(\text{A and B})$$

Probability is usually expressed as a percent, but all math should be completed using decimals.

Statistical Testing

- **Null hypothesis:** a hypothesis of no difference; always the comparator
- ***p*-value:** the probability that results were obtained by chance given that the null hypothesis is true
- **Confidence interval:** a range of values believed to contain the true value with a given level of probability (confidence)

Visual Data Interpretation

- **Graphs:** analyze the axes first to determine whether the scale is linear, logarithmic, or semilog and what the units are. Determine whether relationships are direct or inverse.
- **Pie charts:** compare portions of data to a whole or relative responses of a group
- **Bar charts and histograms:** compare absolute or relative responses between groups
- **Box plots:** contain information about measures of central tendency and distribution; may be comparative or single

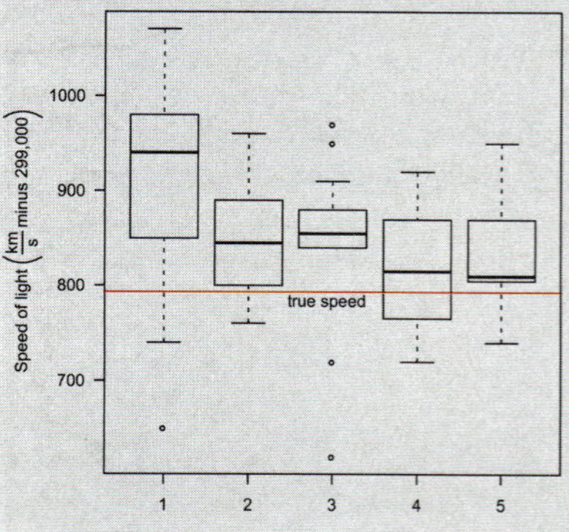